Schuylkill

Valley

Journal

Volume 52

Spring/Summer 2021

Patrons of *Schuylkill Valley Journal*
(contributions of $50 or more)

Subscriptions:
    Single Issue: $10 or $13 (includes mailing)
    1 year: $23 (includes mailing)
    2 years: $45 (includes mailing)

Submissions: See page 158 for a complete list of guidelines.

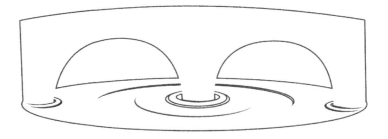

Cover photo: Pennsylvania Railroad War Memorial
Sculptor: Walker Hancock, 1950
Photographer: Ron Howard

Founding Editor . . . . Jim Marinell

Publisher and Editor-in-Chief . . . . Peter Krok

Senior Editor . . . . Mark Danowsky

Poetry Editor . . . . .Bernadette McBride

Fiction Editor . . . . Fran Metzman

Flash Fiction Editor . . . . M.J. Iuppa

Creative Non-Fiction Editor . . . . .Rob Kaniuk

Non-Fiction Editor . . . . .Peter Krok

Art Editor . . . . .David P. Kozinski

Feature Writer . . . . Mike Cohen

Staff Writer . . . . Ray Greenblatt

Contributing Writer . . . . Eric Greinke

Editorial Assistant (Submissions Reader) . . Jenna Geisinger

Online Architect/Producer . . . . Zoe Musselman

Social Media Coordinator . . . . Cleveland Wall

Staff Photographer . . . . Ron Howard

Print Production Editor/Layout Design . . . . Ed Hart

Schuylkill Valley Journal is published twice a year,
and is also available online at
www.svjlit.com

Contents
Volume 52, Spring/Summer 2021

Non-Fiction

Flash Fiction

Fiction

Creative Non-Fiction

AN ANGEL TO REMEMBER

Mike Cohen and Connie Swartzman

We had been here many times, on our way to other places, headed north to Boston or New York, south to Richmond or D.C. Philadelphia's 30th Street Station was generally a means to an end. But this time, it was our destination. Connie and I were here on a mission, a pilgrimage to this venerable residence of the Archangel Michael.

Here we stood in the great concourse, on the marble floor amidst resounding limestone walls, where echoes seem to reflect all the voices that have passed here since 1934. The building was recently restored with adherence to its original style: the Corinthian columns, the Art Deco lighting fixtures that stalactite from the coffered ceiling, the wooden benches that offer respite to weary travelers. The ambient sounds echoed through us in this great building that embodies the spirit of transportation not just to other places, but to other times as well.

Since 1952, a presence that dominates the eastern entrance to the concourse has served as a reminder of Pennsylvania Railroad's contribution to the nation in the war years. To commemorate the employees who lost their lives in the fighting of World War II, railroad officials wanted a memorial featuring a figure of the Archangel Michael lifting the body of a dead soldier.

For this commission, they made the very apt selection of sculptor Walker Hancock, a graduate of the Pennsylvania Academy of Fine Arts and an established and respected artist known for garden and architectural sculptures. He had designed the Air Medal, a military award for meritorious service in aviation. In 1944, Hancock served as one of ten officers sent to Europe in an effort to preserve historical and artistic treasures jeopardized in the conflict. These officers have become better known as the Monuments Men from the film that popularized their story. Hancock's personal involvement in the war added an emotional dimension to his technical qualifications as a war memorial sculptor.

This is a fitting place for an archangel to alight. What other indoor space could so ably accommodate a thirty-nine foot high monument? The sculpture itself is twenty-eight feet high. It depicts the angel upraising the body of a fallen soldier from the fires of battle. The eleven-foot high granite base bears the names of 1,307 Pennsylvania Railroad employees who served and died in World War II. Connie looked up to the dead soldier and the angel whose wings extend upward drawing her gaze toward the ceiling.

"He's not your ordinary cherubic-looking angel," she declared. Indeed, this angel is not of the ilk reputed to dance lightly and invisibly on the head of a pin. This great bronze angel is strong and solemn. From the sturdy legs to the muscular arms to the up-spread wings, this Michael is of a physicality and demeanor suited to his task of uplifting the dead.

Then Connie read the inscription on the black granite base: "In memory of the men and women of the Pennsylvania Railroad who laid down their lives for our country 1941–1945."

After reciting the words, Connie began reading the names, one by one. The echoes got louder.

*

A man sat down next to me and lit a cigar. "You can't smoke in here," I said. He just gave me a strange look, took a puff and let it out. The aroma (if such an odor can be called that) reminded me of my Uncle Jack, who loved a good cigar but smoked a lot of cheap ones.

Cigar Man puffed away. Connie was reading her way through the names inscribed on the monument, as the angel looked on. Soon the smoke became so thick I could not see Connie or the angel. The sounds echoing in the concourse were joined by a loud clacking — a familiar sound, not unlike that of the wheels of a train running on the track. It was the split flap flapping of the Solari board, mechanically updating its display of arrival and departure times. I hadn't heard that sound since my last visit here a few years ago. The Solari board was to have been replaced by a new digital display. There was controversy as many local travelers wanted the Solari board to remain. It was a comfort to hear the familiar sound. I turned toward it, but could not see the board through the smoke in my eyes.

Just as I was about to get up and walk away from the smoking stranger, he spoke. The voice was not of a stranger but of Uncle Jack who'd had the habit of making barely intelligible pronouncements around the cigar in his mouth. I heard in Uncle Jack's muffled diction, the very words he said to me when I was a boy. "So you're the youngest in your family," he said to me, knowing full well there were just my parents and me in the household. "That's a big respon-

sibility, young man." This he had said with a chuckle many years ago. I did not understand the humor or the meaning behind it at the time.

Now, his right hand clasped my shoulder as his left removed the cigar from his mouth, "Being the youngest means you get to be the memory. If you forget it, it's gone. That's a big responsibility."

The Solari board began clacking again. "Hear that?" said Uncle Jack. "Remember that sound. Years from now it will be gone… unless you remember."

*

"That all travelers here may remember those of the Pennsylvania Railroad who did not return from the Second World War." It was Connie reading aloud the inscription on the far side of the memorial. The concourse was quiet, the smoke had subsided. Connie looked up at the angel holding the soldier and saluted. I heard her every footstep as she walked over.

"Without going anywhere," she sighed, "I feel like I've been on a journey."

"I feel as if you've been gone a long while," I said as we hugged.

"So many names," Connie remarked, "so many died so young."

The 1,307 names on the Pennsylvania Railroad War Memorial are only part of the story. There were countless others who took a hiatus from their railroad careers to do a stint in the armed services. Meanwhile, the railroad itself served in the war effort, moving war materials, from bullets to tanks, and transporting troops. It did so despite the decimation of its experienced work force. With so many off to war, most of them men, women were hired to do the jobs men would do in peacetime. Without 'Rosie the Railroader' the country's principal means of transportation would have been crippled, as would have been the war effort itself.

Our fathers had both been in the army in the second World War.

"My dad was on a ship somewhere in the Pacific, headed for Japan," Connie recalled. "But when V-J Day was announced, the ship did a quick about face. What a thrill it must have been for him to find himself on the way back to the United States! The last leg of my father's journey was by train. Years later he told me about it being the happiest homecoming of his life. He loved to remember the astonished and delighted looks on the faces of Uncle Cy, Aunt

Sophie and my mother, when he showed up unannounced at the door, after walking home from the station. I wasn't there, but I can just see him coming up those stairs from the tracks and hurrying through this hall in his uniform with his duffel bag on his shoulder and discharge papers in his hand."

"Strange how you can form a memory of things you never experienced," I said. "It's like time-travel. I guess that's what memorials are about."

Connie looked back at the memorial, the angel reflected in her eyes.

Hand-in-hand we walked through the concourse. I looked up at the digital screen that had replaced the Solari board a couple of years earlier.

"Remember the old noisy message board that used to be here?" Connie murmured, her face lit by the blueish brightness of the big screen above us. "I kind of miss it."

I nodded as we walked through the smoke-free concourse toward the exit.

HERE WE ARE:
AN INTERVIEW WITH GLORIA PARKER

Mark Danowsky: There is an undercurrent of loss, grief, and trauma in many of your poems. Can you discuss how poetry has been a useful space for speaking about your experiences with loss?

Gloria Parker: I think most of what I write is about loss and grief... sometimes with a little humor. I began to write in my twenties, when I was going through a tough emotional time. I wrote, largely because I had to... to try to put into words what was painful, in order to gain some perspective and distance from overwhelming feelings.

MD: Your poems feel very "no nonsense" to me. That is, you do not obfuscate, you are not the "mysterious poet" on the page. How would you like readers to feel in response to such directness in your poems?

GP: I'm glad you see them as "no nonsense." I try to use language that I'd use if I were speaking directly to someone. I try to be honest, hope I'm not too prosy, but I do want my poems to be understandable.

MD: Can you talk about the role of love in your poetry?

GP: I suppose I write more about longing than love. I have loved, of course, and like everyone, lost too. Loss seems to stick closer to me.

MD: Who would you say are influences on your poetic style?

GP: Not so much by what he wrote, but because of the attention he paid me when I was young, the poet Stephen Berg helped me a lot. He would read my poems, take out a red pencil and eliminate what he thought was unnecessary. He even sent them out to journals without telling me. He gave me some needed confidence.

MD: Do you have a sense of what kind of mood you are usually in when you feel the impulse to write?

GP: I'm usually doing something else when I have an idea. I'll stop what I'm doing and begin to write. That's why my laundry might stay in the dryer for days. Sometimes I'll be driving the car and a phrase or image comes and I pull off to the side of the road and look for a receipt from the grocery store to write on.

MD: Who are your favorite poets and writers? Who do you never tire of reading?

GP: I haven't read much of Kenneth Patchen in a long time, but parts of his poems remain and still move me. I love Stephen Dunn. I don't usually feel envious, but his poems make me wish I could write like that! Some others are Szymborska, John Brehm, Linda Pastan, Liesel Mueller, Jane Kenyon, Ron Koertge, and C. K. Williams. There are many more, but these come to mind right now. The novels and short stories of Stephen Millhauser are wonderfully imaginative and fun.

About the Interviewer

Mark Danowsky is a Philadelphia poet, Senior Editor at *Schuylkill Valley Journal*, and EIC of ONE ART: a journal of poetry.

STOPPED

The woman in the car next to mine
sobs and talks to someone who isn't there.
For all I know she's crazy. How could I know?

I might be, myself. I've cried at this light.
I've reached for a hand no one else can see.
Is she angry or bereft? Or both?

Does she dry her eyes before going into work,
pull herself together in Trader Joe's parking lot?
Will sun glasses have to be worn inside?

WHY SHE WRITES

August heat blankets the dank auditorium.
The audience yawns. The poet sags.

She'd barely closed the book on her last ode
when a hand shoots up.

A man asks what sounds more like an accusation
than a question: Why do you write so many poems
about animals?

She could say, *Same reason one writes about trees
or God or politics. Maybe they need to…maybe it's
what they love.*

Instead, she tells him she was raised on a farm,
rose before dawn to milk cows and feed chickens

had a buckskin mare named Frankie,
whose muzzle smelled like sweet corn.

But none of it's true.
She grew up in a row house.

Her animals wore collars with ID tags
and ate from bowls on the kitchen floor.

Yes, she loved them…writes about them
because she can write,

and because words for animals come easier
than words for a lost child.

WHAT I WANT

Long after the autopsy
confirms the cause

I see a silhouette in a car,
an arm, out of the window,

a cigarette held by a hand
I'm sure I'd know anywhere.

And when I follow that boy
into the 7-11 parking lot

he'll step out and turn
a sneering face to mine.

The prayer I didn't even know
I'd uttered goes unanswered

and like any sane person
who knows better

I'll still go on looking
for the face I want to see.

HERE WE ARE

Wading through
Puddles of small talk

Not a thing in common
Can we find.

Whatever made us
Call it love

Must have been a mirage

Something you see
When you're dying of thirst

BOY DOLL

First one I ever saw called to me
from the toy store window.

I had to have him. I begged and sobbed
and swore I'd never ask for anything ever again.

My mother didn't stand a chance.
I worked her over till she cried uncle.
And by late June, he was mine.

I couldn't wait to take off his sailor suit,
see what secrets lay beneath.

Mornings, he sat on my lap at the table.
All day, I dragged him from swing
to slide, to sand box.

I nearly scrubbed the features from his face
in the tub.

I'd tuck him in and kiss him goodnight,
but his eyes didn't close and his hard
rubber hair couldn't be combed.

By September, I'd thrown him over
without even a goodbye.

And love, it seems, still vanishes
the way it did then, without fanfare,
without a trace.

A DOG POEM

Never thought I'd be writing one.
Never wanted a dog.

What's a dog, really,
but a child that never grows up?

Still, I let them talk me into a puppy,
'cause that's what you do for your kids.

Whatever they swore, I knew he'd be
mine when the weather was bad.

TOUCH

Winter's the time to write
about what sleeps poorly.

I close my eyes only to feel
mother's thumb and forefinger
picking imaginary nits out of my hair.

Keats had it right. Touch does
have a memory. And it's hard to kill.

It took me fifteen years to learn
to keep my head out of her hands.

My father's touch and the childhood
it took with it, come back at a will
not my own.

I pin my words to a leafless branch,
to the spectral moon it's bisected.

SLOG

Winter seeps in…
fills the cracks…expands

sleeps in… sleeps poorly,
won't wear clean clothes

comb its hair or wash the dishes.
Winter doesn't remember

to change the sheets
on the bed in which it lies fallow.

It eats cookies… leaves crumbs
and the television on, 24/7.

Winter broods… ruminates,
believes in nothing…

cannot read write or think,
won't answer the phone

go anywhere or give an inch,
till it's over.

Acknowledgments:

"Stopped" first appeared in *The Healing Muse.*

"Why She Writes" first appeared in *Black Coffee Review.*

"Slog" and "Here We Are" first appeared in *Margie.*

"A Dog Poem" first appeared in *Edison Literary Review.*

"Boy Doll" and "Touch" first appeared in *South Florida Poetry Journal.*

BLUEBIRD IN SPRING

Joseph A. Cilluffo

It can't know that I'm the one
who hung the feeder on the pole
that I planted there for just this reason
its curved wrought iron end a swan's neck
or shepherd's crook   the bird surely
can't imagine sitting there
in the cold breeze of early spring
its blue feathers just beginning to deepen
into the darker hue of attraction to find a mate
that I placed the seed out just for it
though it looks at me for a moment
with something like recognition
then flies away   how many times
I've done the same
cast a dark eye backwards
with the fear that we call instinct
the long memory in our bones
and seen only danger   something
prowling along the ground beating
the tall grass to send me
reeling from the outstretched hand
of another animal wanting only
to show me love.

RETURNING FROM A COLLEGE VISIT
ON THE FIRST DAY OF SPRING

Daniel A. Zehner

We drive past the fields and ponds,
Indiana farms, Ohio, Pennsylvania's
hills and woods, snow blowing all day
through the grey sky on the first day of spring,
things better with him since his winter's visit home.

We don't pretend to know whose woods
these are we now pass, nor can we
recall all the lines, the swirling
flurries reminding us of night
and frost before the thaw.

What mysteries occur from talk
and the turning of the earth,
as the dark despair of winter
becomes the yellow hope of spring.

MEDITATION IN THE TIME OF CORONAVIRUS

Joyce Meyers

Would I surrender a ventilator
that keeps me breathing
to save a child's life? Would you?
How to measure, what to weigh?
Maybe consider how many
sunsets I have seen, the dying
of a day blossoming
lavender and rose. Or count
the days and years when someone
loved me. Have I climbed
enough mountains? What about
the taste of chocolate, the sunlight
on a cardinal's wing?

                Does it,
can it, matter if I never write
another poem, taste another peach?
I know it doesn't. I've had
my portion, have no right to cling
despite the body's greed,
the stubborn will of cells
to keep on keeping on. The moral
imperative is clear. So easy
to decide from the comfort
of my living room as I watch
the spring unfold and practice
social distance.

             Through the window
a blue jay on a budding magnolia
branch, a sweet frisson of joy.
A goldfinch brings another.
Should I consent to close
my eyes to gifts like these
to let a child see? No doubt
I should, I know I would,
but not without
a wistful glance behind.

THE RIVER'S WIFE

Francine Witte

Each night, I ask him if he still loves me. He tells me
instead how he started, handfuls of rain and mountain streams,
how it trickled into a muscled flow. I ask him again and that's
when he goes back to hiss and spin. I give up and head home,
lonely, cutting my feet on scraggs of rocks and fallen twigs.

Some nights I wake up, go to the kitchen turn on the faucet
full blast. Waterfingers lacing my own. My father warned me,
said that the river is made up of tears from all the fish that never
made it out to sea. He said he was a river once, a foaming, raging
twist of a man who lured my mother from the banks, how she gave

up, girl-like, to his tumble and roar. How I, myself, am part river,
how if I listen close enough, I can hear the whoosh
that is louder than the beating of my heart.

LOSS WAS THE COLOR OF THE MOON

Aiden Heung

Loss was the color of the moon
above the mountains and she felt it
every night, leaning against the wall,
looking high and far towards the grove
where she had buried him like a seed.
She remembered the upturned earth
unpetalling beside her feet, laying bare
the darkness that looked like fecundity.
But he would not sprout the coming spring
or the next. She had to learn to wrestle
with grief that didn't leave at daybreak.
She had to believe in something.
But I was too young to understand
the afterlife—she kept talking to herself
until sleep wound down a short promise
of peace. And the wind came tenderly,
caressing her hoary tresses of hair
like a good husband.

That was how I remembered her that day,
a woman who sank her body into a chair,
head dropped, her nose twitching slightly.
I hurried to her, for a moment fearing
the inevitable, and stopped
at the shadow of a smile on her face.

BEECH

Elizabeth Fletcher

Winter wind drives against my back
Rushing water bathes my roots
On my silvery branches ice crackles
I lean across Cocalico creek

My heartwood is hollow

At midnight your calls echo
off the cold burning stars
Your bronze feathered wings
brush my bark
Tiger of the night sky

My heartwood shivers

Your mate answers
deep on the night wind
Across the rising moon he sweeps
You whirr and dance
Huntress

My heartwood stirs

Snow drifts against my back
Creek ice blooms under my shadow
My branches whisper
night song
to the three fragile new moons
beneath your feathered cloak

Nestled deep in my heartwood

Some say come spring
a beech leafs out all at once.

OFF-SEASON AT THE SHORE

Ray Greenblatt

I like to watch out the window
a three-day storm
drive against the coast,
making the world gray
turning sky invisible
water against water.

I like to hop on
my old English bike
to wander among millions
of dollars of swank buildings
unpopulated off-season,
but I am here surviving.

One restaurant, one bar
one rickety old theater open
showing only two movies,
as I pound over a hard beach
the surf deafening,
a bat flying out of the moon.

AFTERLIFE

Ray Greenblatt

I go to the place you feel most at home
on that wide desolate beach
where all seems pure and infinite,
wind and sea and sand solid objects
which make up your happiest world
bestowing the peace you seek.

I cast no shadow
simply hover in the air
like a lone thought,
no longer trying to contact
when newly in this state
no longer frustrated

just observing as one
is allowed to do
blessing you as you find
your way as all of us must.
Yet your dog stops to sniff
and stare in the way dogs do.

TIME IS A RABID DOG

Steve Denehan

At first you didn't see it
you were so alive
so quick in your step
that it was far behind you
an indecipherable speck
almost nothing really

you became aware of it later
distant, concentric growls
eyes on you
always on you

later still it came
with such stealth
that when you turned
you saw
only its hot breath
on cold nights

eventually it made its move
the attack wild and brutal
beartrap jaw, steel teeth
foaming mouth, eyes red-brown fury
matted fur on your tongue
as you bit back
again and again and it fell back
again and again
to stalk, hackles raised

now it sits on your lap
a curled heat
a contented rumbling
under your hand
the television is on
but you don't watch it anymore
instead, you gaze out the window
at the November garden
and whimper
at the dry leaves on the grass.

NAME YOUR POISON

(prescription drugs advertised on US television: a found poem)

W. D. Ehrhart

Abilify	Enbrel	Movantik
Aczone	Entresto	Myrbetriq
Adderall	Entyvio	Namenda
Afrezza	Epiduo	Namzaric
Aimovig	Epclusa	Nasonex
Alavert	Eucrisa	Neudexta
Amitiza	Evista	Neulasta
AndroGel	Exelon	Niaspan
Anoro	Farxiga	Nicoderm
Aricept	Fasenra	N. Flexpen
Astepro	Flowmax	Nuedexta
Axiron	Fluad	Nuplazid
Belsomra	Gardasil	Omnaris
Belviq	Harvoni	Onexton
Bexsero	Hetlioz	Onglyza
Beyaz	Humira	Opdivo
Biktarvy	Ibrance	Oracea
Botox	Ilumya	Orlissa
Breo Ellipta	Imitrex	Orencia
Brilinta	Intuniv	Osphena
Brisdelle	Invokana	Otezla
Caduet	Januvia	Ozempic
Chantix	Jardiance	Piqray
Cialis	Jublia	Pradaxa
Contrave	Kerydin	Premarin
Cosentyx	Keytruda	Pristiq
Crestor	Kybella	Prolia
Cymbalta	Latisse	Provenge
Descovy	Latuda	Qbrexza
Dovato	Levemir	Raptiva
Dulera	Linzess	Reclast
Dupixent	Lovaza	Repatha
Effexor	Lyrica	Requip
Eliquis	Mavyret	Restasis
Emgality	Mirapex	Rexulti
Enablex	Mirena	Rozerem

Simponi
Singulair
Skyrizi
Spiriva
Stelara
Symbicort
Taltz
Tamiflu
Tanzeum
Tecfidera
Toujeo
Toviaz
Trelegy

Tremfya
Tresiba
Trilipix
Trintellix
Triumeq
Trulicity
Trumenba
Truvada
Uloric
Vaniqua
Vascepa
Verzenio
Viagra

Viberzi
Victoza
Vraylar
Vyvanse
Xarelto
Xeljanz
Xeomin
Xiaflex
Xifaxan
Xofluza
Yaz
Zicam
Zostavax

Side effects may include constipation, skin rash or dermatitis, dehydration, diarrhea, dizziness, drowsiness, dry mouth, belching, headache, itching, insomnia, nausea, fever, malaise, abnormal heart rhythms, bruising, internal bleeding, blurred vision, cloudy or decreased urine, increased urge to urinate, painful urination, abdominal pain, stomach pain, chest pain, arm pain, jaw pain, back pain, bladder pain, sweating, chills, coughing, ear congestion, nasal congestion, loss of voice, runny nose, sneezing, sore throat, hoarseness, vomiting, loss of appetite, erectile dysfunction, loss of libido, numbness, prickling, indigestion, muscle cramps, swelling, shivering, sleeplessness, confusion, depression, elation, irritability, unsteadiness, inability to concentrate, acid reflux, anaphylaxis, kidney failure, cancer, and suicide.

ON BEHALF OF DANDELIONS

John Grey

As it happens,
even the weeds flower.
Dandelions lead the pack,
a yellow you wish your hair
had retained,
straight sun-seeking stamens
that put your spine to shame.

You're out there with the mower now,
cutting them down,
claiming the cause of neatness
but it is really a jealous rage.

No worry.
Seeds scatter,
burrow into welcoming soil.
They'll be back next year.
And maybe you'll be back next year.
But try saying that with confidence.

PLACE UNKNOWN/KNOWN

Luray Gross

I wish I knew the chamber of the mind,
its deepest caverns, its Chapel of Lions,
its Galerie du Fond, but I've rarely gone
beyond the prehistoric entrance,
never shimmied on my belly

in the dark and mud to press
through the Crawling Passage.
Instead I read of those
amazed by the curled bison
on the ceiling of Altamira–

its ochre hue, its looming power,
the aurochs in the Hall of Bulls
in Lascaux. That's what I'm going
to do today, after I lower the lid
of this laptop. I'll travel to France

on wings of words, unworried
about what I might find were I
to close my eyes and let my
monkey mind hold sway. If I were
to follow each strand of thought,

leap with it across canyons,
not fearing in the least the raging
stream below, would I know any more
about that gray and seemingly
undefined mass of nerve and charge?

Perhaps never, but tonight
I'll enter the dream world
with a guide as eloquent as Virgil,
and be schooled again by seeing, feeling,
what I cannot know by day.

THE LURE OF RUINS

Joyce Meyers

Blank eyes that once
were windows in a crumbling
stone façade. Behind, a hint
of hearth, a creek beyond.
Before it, weeds, barbed wire,
a warning sign to passers-by:
Danger, Keep Off.
But why?

Something seductive lingers
about decay, a whiff
of history unspoken, of soup
in an iron pot over an open fire,
babies birthed, cuddled,
mourned, smell of sweat,
bits of earth stuck
to calloused hands.

It matters little that the house
holds not a hint of beauty,
designed as it was by the architect
of necessity, no eye for anything
but shelter from sun and storm.
Time is a clever sculptor,
softening rough-hewn stone,
carving shapes that sing

of stars and seasons. And what
do we, with easels and cameras
poised, hope to capture from
the secrets of these stones?
Between the crevices, a random
seed dropped by a bird
migrating north to breed

will become an infant garden,
invisible now but to the soul
that feels the pull. Like curious
children who can't resist the urge
to touch, to climb, to turn a stone
or two, we are seduced
by silent promise
in what is left behind.

SENTRY DUTY

Ray Keifetz

Everywhere empty pedestals,
angry voices: revenge
upon stones
that can't be mended.
No more lilacs
slipping from our hands.
No more infants
nesting on the branches.
Granite sentries without a leg,
without a face—
Lay the wreaths,
sing the names,
sweep, weed, seed the deaf
dumb graves.
You were kinder
when you dug them.

AFGHANISTAN

William Heath

Our troops in Afghanistan
are issued hip-waders
where there are no marshes,
a chain saw fit for logging
in a land bare of trees.
Their mission to kill the Taliban,
a name that means student.
To the commanders the war
is a box to check, a step
up the career ladder,
for soldiers it is one more
body bag to fill, another road
where bombs do not fall
from the sky but are planted
underground like monstrous
lethal blooms, or concealed
by objects that appear
harmless. The real mission:
chasing ghosts in the deserts,
ghosts in the mountains,
while those ghosts keep
our troops in their sights from
village roofs, roadside ambushes.
"Two to the heart and one
to the head" the joke goes,
a mission accomplished.

THE QUARRY INSIDE YOU

Nicole Greaves

Each day now is a Sunday, the other side of what happened,
that huskiness of goodbye—

even when I say I am happy, I am
not, but pushing myself to believe, and it has to be enough,

like the way I hear you, from the well, that quarry
that is all an immigrant has of her dream,

the hole of it which becomes a life
in that symmetry of a thing and its absence.

WHAT THEY NEVER TALK ABOUT

Mark Robinson

What they never talk about
is the milk spilt from the plastic jug
and how it mixes with her blood
inside the roof of the upside-down car.

It's her singing voice, her favorite bird (humming),
how she was the type of woman
content to hang the laundry on a line outside to dry—
things they say about my mother.

Trauma is the beginning of heartbreak,
is the beginning of fever, is the beginning
of faith.

It took a long time to get her from the arms
of a man I didn't know, pointing into the distance
I could not see.

ON FERRY ROAD

—for my sister, Susan

Lynn Fanock

You're not familiar with the area or the cemetery,
but I think you'd appreciate the setting:
fieldstone walls shaded by oak and pine.
While driving along the road, I can look over
and see your headstone.

When I woke this morning, I recalled
telling you about the deep plum tulips
I recently planted on the berm in my yard.
What do you suppose this means?

Do you remember the time we strode into
Bonwit Teller, bought those matching green striped
dresses, and treated ourselves to lunch at Trader Vic's?
Well, I came across the dress while cleaning out your place.
I can't believe you still had it.

I came along with you to your interview at the WTC,
and on the way out the interviewer offered both of us jobs.
On the subway home, I couldn't imagine working in NYC.
You thrived on its currents and gusts of excitement.
I still prefer peaceful, open landscapes.
Our backyard is practically a wildlife sanctuary!

This morning, I saw a group of fawns frolicking.
They sprinted over the gully and into the neighboring field,
then poof—vanished into the oak and ash.
This afternoon, I bought a bunch of daisies
from CVS to place on your grave.

LAUNDRY

Jennifer L. Freed

A week later,
staring absently

out the kitchen window, past
the clothes line, its billows
of color,

past the white plastic chairs
where he'd sit beside her on warm evenings,

she said to her daughter,

> "I kept looking
> for the bottom sheet.

> It didn't occur to me they would use it
> when they took him.

> But of course they did.

> They took
> my fitted sheet."

WIDOW

Jane Ebihara

it wasn't supposed to end like this
he is supposed to be at the kitchen door
dripping with garden gifts
Sweetness, where'd you put the hummer food?

he gardens still
down at the Prairie City cemetery
where bagpipe strains of *Amazing Grace*
hang heavy in the country air

gardens now like that giant
composter he loved
that sits under the pine tree doing its quiet work

his ragged fishing cap still hangs
on the hall tree hook
and the tracks of his garden boots paint
the floor in front of his favorite chair
the one in which the cat now curls alone
selfish with sorrow

no use shaking a fist at God
she curses him instead
head bowed in the rose garden
the sweet pea patch   the calla lilies—
the white ones he took with him to the grave

curses him with fists of weeds
damn you   it wasn't supposed to end like this
tears are not enough to do this work.

WHAT THEN?

Jennifer L. Freed

Ship of bone and breath and flesh—
but what
when the mast bends like rubber,
when the rudder floats away,
when the wheel spins loose as a toy?

What
when the mind thinks "walk,"
and the foot you feel moving exactly
as it used to
is, in fact, dragging—the floor rising
again to greet your waving palms?

What
do you make of yourself
then,
when the body—your familiar
body, ceases
to be the vessel of your intentions,
becomes, instead, your anchor?

AFTER THE HEART ATTACK

Marsha Foss

> *Tender: noun (nautical)*
> > *a vessel attendant on another, ferrying supplies between ship*
> > *and shore*
> *Tender: adjective*
> > *frail, sensitive, gentle, easily crushed*

God preserve me,
God of gentleness
and sweet,
preserve me
from collecting
Valentine shapes of painted
wood with sentimental tripe
or porcelain hearts too easily
shattered.
I want instead an anchor – stone, perhaps,
cracked and chipped
like my own life,
solid.

I am a tenderfoot at loving,
only lately
attending
to my damaged heart
as I would an ailing child,
and even now
a yearning grows
to tend to other brittle things
or those with broken wings.

Now a vessel on uncharted sea,
I'm lost.
Surprised by swells
and billows
I ferry in supplies, new needs,
releasing dying dreams into the deeps.

I never knew
until its random beats
revealed how sound
and dear
a weakened thing can be.

DISTANCES

Ann E. Michael

We correspond after many years
    the same kinds of jokes.
We like each other, always did
    though we've less in common than ever.
Field behind my house reveals, today
    half a dozen whitetails
oak leaves the color of deer among stones.

Your apartment windows frame the city
    never dark, except in blackouts.
We were lovers in Brooklyn once—
    the blackout thrilled and frightened me.
Less at stake then. No field to steward,
    no property taxes or maintenance fees.

Now we've each paid off our mortgages.
    What does that make us? Privileged?
True, you've had the better career
    almost earning the money you wanted
while I fled the city's surge and crush.
    How bored you would feel watching clouds,
deer, getting your good shoes dirty.

But the sort of person who uses the word
    epistemological, spelled correctly,
in a text message—that brings a smile.
    It's only when you see a photo of
my grown children that you write: *How long ago that was,*
    how young we were.

AGING IN PLACE

Linda M. Fischer

Looking at the lichen-chapped maple
out back, it strikes me that as I approach
another decade, I, too, am aging in place—
or trying to—along with my appliances.
First, the dishwasher elected to take early
retirement—on the cusp of a festive Easter
dinner! Then, two stove-top burners just
upped and quit. For weeks I'd been watching
the slow onset of Alzheimer's creep up
on my botvac, which was losing its sense
of direction and beginning to transmit
a fruitless robotic message at regular
intervals, thus raising my level of anxiety.
Would it need an organ transplant
or should I consign it to an early grave?
My pappy would have said it's only money.
But is it? Lately, my life has been fraught
with too many decisions—and challenges.
As I wait for the battery I finally ordered,
I fret about installing and re-calibrating it.
Symptomatic of advancing age, I'm told.
What to do? Well, I opted to treat myself
and got my nails done in a trendy blue.

ANNE SEXTON AND THE ROLE OF WOMEN

Catherine Findorak

I was introduced to you in a poetry class, junior year.
The professor was an old man. He found the textbook holy.
We read a lot of dead men in class, but I wrote a paper on you.
You and I, we both felt too much.

Winter was nipping around the edges of me, the lonely transfer student.
Dead and gone, nailed to the page, you were one thing I could talk to.

I wrote until I believed what I was saying:
that in your poems one could see the way being a woman
was crucial to your despair. With an animal body and babies to feed,
you were a difficult woman, saying too much again.

In his office the professor asked me if I was having thoughts of suicide.
I told him I was fine, that your poems were a bit intense.
I walked across the campus afterwards, embarrassed at the way
my pain seeped through me, into everything I did.

Ten years later I've got dishes in the sink, bills to pay.
I plant vegetables in the backyard. I hope for the future.

That's a different kind of pain I avoid writing down.
The difference between you and me now is I'm wondering if
the world will die with me clinging to it, trying to grow old.

MUTED

Nancy Smiler Levinson

From his right screen webinar window
the adult-ed teacher asks if everyone
can see the photo he has put up

Yes yes you nod at your desk
while he refers to a small dark figure
among a hoard of mustachioed men
yes yes I see her you murmur

That is Marie Curie, he says,
circling her with a tiny red light
She's a mere speck you say aloud

In his remote class Mr. Lipsky
neither hears nor sees you   yet how eagerly
you sit in conversation with him
and the other registered students
whoever they may be

During a short break you stretch and circle a bit
nibble an oreo cookie   strangely recalling
a scene from your childhood   age three or four

sitting next to a radio   a forties-style radio
mesh webbing   a little girl named Baby Snooks
is talking to you from inside the wooden box
and you are chattering back to her

delighted in banter with another little girl
while your mother is upstairs feeding infant twins
and outside is blowing a forbidding snowstorm.

THE NEIGHBORHOOD GNOMES APPLY FOR HOMESCHOOL ACCREDITATION

John Wojtowicz

The towering evaluator was welcomed inside by a rosy-cheeked
matriarch who was quickly informed
that her homeschool curriculum
did not meet minimum academic standards.

The pencil-skirted specialist contended
that gardening was not a supplement
for earth science and that playing pan flute on a toadstool
was not sufficient for music education.

She continued that mending a bluebird's
wing would not qualify as anatomy
and examining tree rings
didn't meet the benchmarks for world history.

The stern-faced woman did seem struck
by the craftsmanship of the children's geometric
bird houses but made clear
there was nothing common core about them.

When asked about Language Arts,
the father proudly trotted out their middle child
in green-peaked cap and braids who
seamlessly recited *When I Heard the Learn'd Astronomer.*

The assessor tapped her clipboard with a pencil
seemingly unimpressed and reminded
the beaming would-be-educators
the syllabus specifically suggested *Song of Myself.*

DEAR H.D.,

Katherine Falk

Let's say we're stuck in the extreme fuddle predicted
by the Mayans: alternating 5,000-year cycles: Savagery,
Civilization, Savagery; that we completed a 5,000-year cycle
of civilization just 20 years ago; perhaps a why for how
it's come to this, our darkened sky that lost sight of its own sun
and moon, as sublunar factions prevail.

Where are you now, HD, and can your knowing be channeled
to move us beyond the savagery tunnel we're in, on our stomachs
in the mud without fresh air? Can your ideas move us to life sacred
on a daily basis to light, the way you took religion and squeezed
all the visions into one, propelled theories and fancies out
to the multiverse to orbit outside time's clatter to create something

new, to eliminate war-igniting feuds, life that can be trusted.
Now, as neighbors forget that they are neighbors, as poison vines
grow hardier, send out venom, extend their threatening reach,
as people wail for a potion, an amulet to cure the ills,
I sit in the same Quaker meetinghouses you did with silence deep
as a well we descend by ladder to a crossroads of continents

a desert, spanned by our worried ancestors and our willing
descendants, all reminding the sun to ignite itself
again and piece the shattered horizon back together,
each beehive of space: a person that lived, lives, or will live,
lined up to lighten the dark, appreciating as you did
the wandering stars, the habit of the lovely fixed ones.

ON THIS ISSUE'S POEMS:

You might have noticed a number of our poems in this issue bear a direct relation to longing, hope, illness, and death —or at least a peripheral brush with these— even those which speak of spring and new life. Reading through the submissions, I couldn't help considering how much the pandemic has informed, at a cellular level, our collective psyche; generated a lens through which we've taken to viewing daily life with its many adjustments over this past year, its reminders of what we already know when it comes down to it: that all we have, in reality, is just this one day we're in right now as we read this.

I remember a teacher telling us in class long ago, "If not for love and loss and death, there would be no poetry." It seems this has proven true even more in our current era than when she first said it. But just as deep winter manages to offer her beauties, however severe, so too does great poetry, however stark its mirror.

—Bernadette McBride
Poetry Editor

EIGHTEEN LINES

Two years ago I told my best friends, a hetero married couple I'd known for close to fifty years, that I'm a trans person. They weren't surprised. They said they'd known for twenty-five years and had just been waiting for me to say something. A year later, the day the husband and I both turned sixty-seven, he told me I really needed to "invest in a training bra, or something, because you kind of look like a seventh grade girl who's starting to, you know … grow." I said I'd go put something on under my polo shirt, smiling all the way to my room to rummage through my suitcase. They had been two of the first I'd spoken to in what came to be an eighteen-month-long coming out journey to nearly all of my friends and many in my family. As anyone who has done that knows, it is terrifying, because no matter how confident you are in believing these people you have known most, or all, of your life will still love you and accept you, there is always that nagging doubt you could be wrong, and they'll leave. It happens; though, fortunately, only twice for me.

Six months after the birthday incident, I was offered a part in a regional theater charity performance of Eve Ensler's play, "The Vagina Monologues." I was to be one of three trans women performing the segment titled, "They beat the girl out of my boy … or so they tried." Coming out to those I knew was difficult, but I still felt a sense of control, as everyone agreed to keep the news among those I told, because I was still only "semi-out;" "semi" because I couldn't be out at work and had yet to tell my elderly and very conservative parents. But the play, performing in front of 300 people I didn't know, was going to be something altogether different; the illusion of control would vanish entirely. For the first time ever, I was going to be truly open to the world, just Catherine, not anyone else.

After my first pass through the script, I wondered if I was the best person for this play because I felt it wasn't my story. It was a story that definitely needed to be told, just not mine. I don't know why I thought that; maybe I just didn't want to remember the years of hiding and lying. Or, maybe, I felt guilty because so much of this hadn't happened to me. I was elated when I was assigned these lines:

> *Got my first hormone shot*
> *Got permission to be myself[1]*

The feminine is in your face
I lift my eyebrows more
I'm curious
I ask questions[2]

Of all the lines in the segment, I felt so comfortable with these, because they were me, even though my "first" wasn't a shot; it had been a pill, taken on my 64th birthday while sitting in my living room and holding my wife's hand. Those words spoke to a giant change in the lives of many other trans women, changes they had desperately wanted to make, to stop hiding behind a false masculine image. For me, though, it had just been raising a translucent veil that never really hid who I truly was if you knew me well enough and paid attention. My hiding had been in plain sight and to my friends, those thoughts or just feelings made sense now. And to myself, I made sense now.

Rehearsal was the first time in my life when I participated in an event where I knew no one and they all only knew me as Catherine. There were eighteen of us; a few who had acting experience, most who did not, and a few who were petrified at even the thought of speaking to an audience. But they all thought this play was more important than their fears. They were to be the voices of the voiceless, and they welcomed me as one of those voices, as well. No one looked at me askance or mis-gendered me. I was, in their eyes, fully female. In fact, conversations were no different from what they would be at any party or gathering I'd ever attended had I been born female. "You're a teacher? Tell me about that? How is it teaching young kids these days? That's a really pretty dress. I love your earrings, where'd you get them?" I was truly myself, nothing hidden, no acting, no affected voice or concern about the length of my hair. I was just me, all of me, and they embraced me immediately. It was, in a word, affirming.

Eve had written this monologue for five voices, but realizing finding five trans women might be difficult, the director was given the latitude to assign lines based on the number of voices available. There were three of us, and at our first rehearsal (we only had two) we took turns reading different lines, so the director could decide which lines to assign to each of us. The first three times through our part of the script, I did not read the final passage, eighteen lines that were not me, lines that frightened me, lines that required so much more than I thought I had within me to give. When the director finally asked me to read them on our last pass, it was all I could do to muster any voice at all.

I live now in the female zone
but you know how people feel about
immigrants.
They don't like it when you come from someplace else.
They don't like it when you mix.

They killed my boyfriend
They beat him insanely as he slept
With a baseball bat
They beat this girl
Out of his head.

They didn't want him
Dating a foreigner
Even though she was pretty
And she listened and was kind.
They didn't want him falling in love
With ambiguity.
They were scared he'd get lost.
They were that terrified of love. [3]

After rehearsal ended, the director said she would look through the entire segment and work out how she wanted to pare five voices to three, and would send us an email with our parts in a few days. That was Sunday. On Tuesday I was assigned not only the lines I felt spoke about me, but the last eighteen, as well.

Eve interviewed scores of trans women before writing this monologue. Everything she wrote was said by one of those women, even the last eighteen lines. Everything is true. Even the last eighteen lines. True. There are people in this world (in the play those swinging the bat were soldiers) who not only want to kill me because I am trans, because I am an "immigrant," but also someone I love, who just might, against all odds, love me, too. I have always known this sort of hatred exists. I hear it nearly every day in the news, in conversations with people who don't know about me as I move through the world even today in stealth mode. I know I have no legal protections to keep my job if I'm found out. In many states, if I were dating and surprised my companion with my "trans ness," and he "lost control" because of fear and killed me, the "trans panic" defense would justify the homicide. I have even heard the loathing from the pulpit of my own church, not from my minister, but from a church member who garnered applause and support for his comments.

Eighteen lines brought screaming home to me everything I have to fear. Eighteen lines brought a woman I'll never know into my arms, wanting to comfort her from thirty years away for the unfathomable pain of her loss. But there was just one line that voiced something I didn't know until I read it aloud:

> *They were that terrified of love.*

Was that it? Were they terrified of us, all of us who are trans, all of us who dare to admit we have been created this way, only because we have all been taught not to love something defined as "different?" Is this why it has been so hard to learn to love myself?

On the night of the play, I held my script in front of me (we all had to read from our own copy of the play, even though most of us knew the words), and I became her. To be sure, I shed tears as I read, and there was a break in my voice as I remembered a violent death I'd not known until I'd read the script the week before. And we, the woman from thirty years ago and I, tried to tell them, the audience and my fellow actresses, why it had happened, what she had finally figured out, but that's so hard to do in just eighteen lines, in just one line. I hope they understood. When I finished there was just silence.

The applause came some moments later, but my time had been suspended. I was standing there with her. She wasn't saying anything; she was just there. I felt her drawn back to a moment she had never left. There were two of us now, not one. She stepped a bit away, and I was left forever changed. I thought back then to what had been my trauma before, and I cried, embarrassed by the comparison. I warmed, smiled and cried at the miracle of friendship in being told to buy a training bra at 67. The applause faded, not because it had ended, but because there was no room for it, as the entirety of my life crashed in instantly, almost crushing the breath out of me, as I realized how much I owed this woman and all of those like her, unimaginably brave all. Eighteen lines, ninety-four words. I was forever changed. Light beckoned me from shadow.

Catherine Glenn
April 23, 2020

1 Ensler, Eve, "The Vagina Monologues", VDay February 2020, Dramatist's Play Service, Inc., NYC, NY (2020) "They beat the girl out of my boy ... or so they tried" "Woman 5" pg. 15.

2 *Ibid.*, "Woman 1" pg. 16.

3 *Ibid.*, "Woman 1" pg. 17.

AMERICAN HISTORIES BY JOHN EDGAR WIDEMAN

A Review

Ray Greenblatt

I first came across John Edgar Wideman's name when I was attracted by a novel title, *Philadelphia Fire* (1990). Leafing through the pages I couldn't help but notice a poetic fire in the prose. As far as I know, Wideman has published no book of poetry. However, in this newest book of short stories *American Histories* (2018) I will look at the poetics in several of them.

I—Family

Wideman has written memoirs about his family, but this book of stories he chose to call fiction. So we must be careful not to assume that these characters were actual. However, from my research they are very close to reality in many ways.

In the story "Maps and Ledgers," the narrator describes his mother: "My mother, from childhood to womanhood, an infectious curiosity, a sense of not starting over but starting fresh, let's go here, let's do this, not because she had mastered a situation or a moment previously but because uncertainty attracted, motivated, formed her." We can readily see the poetic looseness of his sentences; run-ons as well as fragments abound.

In another story, "Bonds," we see the possibly same mother again at the time of the narrator's birth. "She keeps him inside not because she knew the baby, a he, not because she knew she'd be closer to the end of her life once his life begins!" She does not want him born on Friday the 13th.

Then the narrator jumps years in time. "Not because she knew his eyes the last eyes to see her alive. Him silent on a hospital chair beside her hospital bed, book in his hands, monitor beep-beep-beeping, his eyes on a page the precise instant she's no more, missing her last breath." His onomatopoeia is powerful here.

His grandmother had beautiful handwriting. "Letter after letter perfect as eggs. Perfect as print. But better. Her hand cursive. Letters flow like alive things that grow. One growing live into or from the other whether connections visible or not."

His Aunt May was entirely different. "May got loud, raunchy, or ignorant at family gatherings. May, tumbler of whiskey held down with one hand on the armrest pad of her wheelchair while the hand at the end of her other arm points, wiggles, summons all at once, a gesture synced with a holler, growl, and mm-mm, boy, you better get yourself over here and gimme some sugar." Notice the tense shift and the injection of vernacular.

The narrator recalls how as a youth he teased his younger brother. "To fill emptiness where maybe he'd always felt homeless or smothered or locked down in spaces like the ones I allowed him . . . I could have let myself be satisfied with seeing Gene, convinced myself I was saying goodbye to a stranger in Atlanta, but it was him, his neat, pencil-thin mustache, elegant features, my brother's unbegrudging silence in the open casket." ("My Dead") Again, the time leap is shocking as well as poignant.

The narrator shares the loss of a father with a friend who recently lost his. "Him puffy-faced, spiky hair askew, wearing a Peanuts pj top and sweatpants, me in cutoffs, T-shirt, standing in the hall . . . two upper-middle-class, differently colored, orphaned males—could hug." ("Dark Matter")

The family did have its troubles. "That same colored lawyer one day would say to me, shaking his head and reaching out and placing his hand on my shoulder, Family of poor old Aeschylus got nothing on yours, son."

The question seems to be how does one combat the government for the sake of individual freedoms. "How many alive only an instant in these killing fields before they are gone forever. How many does it take to disturb the frozen quiet, black glisten of empire. To penetrate, agitate, produce movement. Not the empire's dead invisible carcass thrashing darkly." ("Writing Teacher") His use of a series, in this case of infinitives, is effective.

II—Bridge

Wideman, as we can see, effectively brings people to life. He also works well with things like the Williamsburg Bridge that becomes the setting for the story. "Pale reds and mottled pinks of my tongue as I wag it at myself each morning in the mirror. Iron fences with flaking paint that's cotton-candy pink frame the entrance to the bridge." ("Williamsburg Bridge") A sharp comparison between mouth of the person and the bridge.

Comparing the bridge to the Statue of Liberty: "In the haze where sky meets sea and both dissolve, a forest of tall cranes and derricks, arms canted at the exact angle of the Statue's arm, return her victory salute."

And beneath flows the East River. "Water colors differently depending on point of view, light, wind, cosmic dissonance. Water shows all colors, no color, any color from impenetrable oily sludge to purest glimmer." Wideman often plays with paradox.

The man on the bridge contemplating suicide mulls the meaning of words. "Posterity, Pentecost, old-fashioned words hoisting themselves up on crutches, rattling, sighing their way through alleys and corridors of steel girders, struts, trusses, concrete piers. Noisy chaos of words graffitied on the pedestrian walkway." This series of nouns especially about the sea echoes some lists Walt Whitman made while writing in Camden, New Jersey.

Concerned about the unstopping machine of time, the distraught man animates his words. "I struggle to open a parenthesis and hold it open, keep a space uncluttered, serene, safe. Me inside it able to gather my thoughts, my words before they disintegrate, before the machine whirs on."

His thoughts are contorted. "Thoughts which smash like eggs on the unforgiving labyrinth's walls. Can I scrape off dripping goo. Twist it into a string to lead me out of whitespace." He wrestles with his decision to jump; he might become a smashed egg, simply goo—vivid metaphors.

In another story his thoughts become bubbles. "At first only a few people noticed transparent clouds passing by with words inside. Then rumors became viral awareness. Imagine capsules in comic books floating above heads of animals or human beings to indicate they are talking and thinking." ("Yellow Sea")

His memories might refer to a soldier in battle. "Color deeper than midnight blue. Dark, scathing, grudging color of a colored soldier's wound coloring dirty white bandages wrapped around his dark chest. An almost total eclipse of color while dark blood slowly drip drop drip drops from mummy wrap into the snow." The repetition of "color" intensifies the gruesome analogy.

Some memories are too painful to deal with. "Silence of a search party standing at the edge of a vast lake after the guide who's led them to it points and says the missing one is out there somewhere. Silence because we've already plunged, already groping in the chill murkiness, holding our breath, dreading what we'll recover or not from the gray water."

III—History

Wideman is also adept at bringing Black history into the living present. He creates a scenario where Frederick Douglass and John Brown converse. Douglass recalls when he was considered no more than "a piece of animated chattel curiously endowed with speech." ("JB & FD") He later grew to become a lover: "He strokes and soothes and quiets and fine-tunes his new young wife's hair and pale skin." Also a forceful leader: "He waves away the noise and stirs it, conducts it, loves it."

But the larger portion of this story focuses on John Brown. When young he was deeply impressed by a frontier wife. "Deep kindness and deep fear hide inside her busyness." But he is more greatly moved by seeing how a slave boy is treated. "Nothing but rags, a dark mound of rags the wind has blown into the house." "A piece of night, ash, cinder trying to stay warm in a corner where it lands."

For John Brown the road he travels can be "a seemingly unending length of rough fabric from the road's coarse thread, then a seamless, silky ride." In another story the road "seems to enter a tunnel that continues endlessly beyond its circular mouth of shadow and floating spots of light, path obscured or consumed or both by unstill brightness and darkness, a path no longer on the ground, but hovering in air." ("Expectations") A fantastic quality is connected to roads.

Brown goes through a kind of metamorphosis seeing so many injustices. "John Brown thinks of it as molting. His feathers shed. A change of color. Him shriven. Cleansed. Pale feathers giving way to darker. Darker giving way to pale." His identification with the oppressed is deep. Another man is named for John Brown: "Time is trouble, time full of trouble, and time on your hands when your hands ain't doing right fills up your time with trouble."

At the end of the story the author thinks of these two famous men as trees. "Trees with thick, ancient-looking gray trunks, bark deeply furrowed as old John Brown's skin, multiple trunks entwined, branches big as trunks, twisted, tortured . . . for a small instant I'm inside them, and it lasts forever." Another poetic technique Wideman employs is to enter a fictional scene.

In "Nat Turner Confesses" he learns to read: "D for Dread. Dream. Did. Dirty. Deed." Ingenious play with letters. Nat is also is concerned with names. "The names they happened to bear when I was born had been passed out like tools passed out to field hands to serve their masters." Wideman deals with names in other stories. "Different and same. Like your name when it's said by someone who speaks a foreign language." ("Lines") "Names are strands of cloth wrapped round us, round the earth so everything doesn't shiver and die of cold."

A man named Thomas Gray has written a phony confession for Nat Turner that he would never say. Instead this man "must listen to every word I brew now, words scourging him, words streaming, stinging up from my belly to my heart to my silent mouth this morning."

Wideman creates a surreal scene mixing history with our present age. "We did it. Made a Nat Turner movie and everyone promises it's a hit. On top for once. Let me tell you it hasn't been easy. Making a movie not a cakewalk."

IV—Strands

The title for this closing section sounds a bit like some of John Edgar Wideman's short story titles—"Wail"—"Snow"—"Bonds." But that is not a misnomer. Since poetic nuggets might be lodged in a certain story, I wish to end by revealing them.

He often lends substantial objects a special aura. "Quiet rain falling in a city never visited before can transform that city's foreignness into intimacy." A poetic view we, perhaps, had felt but never verbalized before.

"The rug's elaborately woven prayers." If an object is created by hand, one's art, if not soul, becomes part of it. It also reminds me of Somerset Maugham's belief that we weave our rug of life and only at our death do we turn it over to discern the pattern.

In this almost sci-fi story "Empire," Givers rule the empire; Gratefuls are controlled by their cell phones. "Why would anyone wish to believe imaginary work or imagined works soundlessly spoken into a device might actually construct a different Empire than the only one necessary and true."

Here is another poetic truth we may have never considered in the story "Expectations." "I expect to miss my right hand if I lose it. Expect my left hand, if I lose my right hand, not to miss it. The parts of my body strangers to one another."

Wideman is concerned with people who get left behind in life because of poverty and lack of education. He takes a movie character named Precious to imagine she immolates herself. "Dust and ashes of Precious a load. Her absence a load. Precious gone, never be back. Weight not gone. We must bear the weight of her death, weight of our lives."

We might learn about the world and ourselves by sound. "Perhaps sounds will clarify the world's shape. Transform me the way sound's magic turns noise to music. I'll be transparent to myself. Present and absent as I listen. Hear answers to an unanswerable question." ("Shape the World Is In")

"Same wish that motivates me some mornings to sit in the bathroom and listen for sounds, for silences telling me I am not the silence that surrounds me. Signs that assure me I possess a shape that belongs to me, and it can poke its way through silence, get on with a life." Philosophy becomes poetry through reality.

Another example of Wideman's poetic imagination: "I pull out her drawer and my wife's inside it, miniaturized, perfectly believable." ("Examination") Here in this final flight of fancy is a rhythm you can hear pulsing as true as a heart: "As if living and questioning never ends, as if a simple question might stump time, buy time, stop time long enough for a boy, a man, to slip past the conductor and ride back and forth to Pittsburgh on a beam of light without paying the price of a ticket." ("Collage")

A DYING EMBER ON THE STEINBECK TRAIL

Mike Dillon

Even from the street the set-up looked dodgy. I turned off the ignition and stared.

"Are you sure?" my wife asked.

"I am now. Look."

I nodded towards the John Steinbeck statue in the front yard, flanked by red bougainvillea and overgrown bushes luxuriating in the September morning sun. The gold painted, life-sized figure wore a double-breasted suit, right hand clasping a book, left hand at rest upon the midsection. The statue looked less like Steinbeck than a grandiloquent, French provincial mayor addressing a captive audience.

There was no need to double-check our self-guided Steinbeck tour map—"Compliments of the City of Pacific Grove." I was first out of the car. Our boys in the backseat were next.

"Whoa," our youngest muttered.

Broken masonry lined the walkway. Sections of a weary, white-painted iron fence sagged towards the street. The cottage curtains were drawn.

My eyes moved upwards: A square, wooden cupola topped by a Pegasus weathervane squatted on the roof, hugely disproportionate to the cottage itself. In architectural parlance, the feature, which included a narrow viewing platform on all four sides, is called a widow's walk—supposedly an add-on for worried wives who would scan the harbor for their returning husbands.

From 1915 to 1918 this had been the cottage of Elizabeth Hamilton, John Steinbeck's maternal grandmother and model for a major character in "East of Eden." Steinbeck and his brother-in-law built the small workroom attached to the cottage.

I motioned to my wife and two boys to follow. Rare, first editions of John Steinbeck's books were supposed to be available for viewing inside. And so, in September 2004, I knocked.

A flutter of commotion broke out inside. I could make out a pair of hurried male voices, furniture scraping across the floor. A man's voice boomed with theatrical, faux-British politeness, "One moment… please."

And the door opened.

* * *

John Steinbeck (1902-1968), author of thirty-three books and winner of the 1962 Nobel Prize for Literature, occupied an honored place in our family. Our two boys, 21 and 18, loved his writing from an early age. We figured this was to be our last road trip together from our Puget Sound home ground. We wanted to return to Monterey and Pacific Grove as a family one more time.

In his Nobel acceptance speech, Steinbeck stated: *Literature is as old as speech. It grew out of human need for it and it has not changed except to become more needed. The skalds, the bards, the writers are not separate and exclusive. From the beginning, their functions, their duties, their responsibilities have been decreed by our species.*

Steinbeck's words shed light on how our youngest, when he was eleven years old, appeared from his bedroom weeping one winter Sunday afternoon. He held "Of Mice and Men" in both hands. He'd just come to the end of the last page.

I've loved the cleanness of Steinbeck's prose; his exact, calligraphic glance that rendered a landscape, a mood, a person in quick strokes. Here's his description of Doc in "Cannery Row," modeled on his friend Ed Ricketts: "He wears a beard and his face is half Christ and half satyr and his face tells the truth."

Steinbeck's stories played out in the full light of the day, but many had their roots nourished in darker, mythic beginnings. His democratic tenderness for the American grain, with a small "d," is a grace note in American letters. He knew that all stories, even the fall of Troy, are local.

The day he won the Nobel Prize for Literature, Steinbeck was asked if he felt he deserved it.

'Frankly, no," he answered.

* * *

A tall figure held the door open, made a half-bow with a sweep of an arm, and invited me in. To my right, in the dim light of the disheveled living room, a compact shadow of a man stuffed a partly-full, bomber-sized bottle of beer behind the sofa and disappeared up the stairs without looking back.

My eyes jumped back to my host.

"You have Steinbeck first editions? It's OK to see them?"

"I do. And you are most welcome to see them."

Richard was a still-handsome man with white, receding hair, his fleshy face lightly stubbled with gray. In his late seventies, maybe. The two top buttons of a dingy white shirt were open to reveal the gold medallion strung around his neck. Shirt tails hung over gray slacks. His outsized gestures were those of an amateur actor never out of character.

Richard motioned me to the beat-up sofa where I dutifully sat. An enlarged photo on the wall showed Richard receiving a blown-up check from a smiling Bill Murray—$1,000, as I recall. The living room table was repository to a plastic knight's helmet with visor painted gold, a plastic white stone with a gold-painted plastic sword stuck in it, stacks of old books, browned newspapers and *Life* magazines. Magazine and newspaper photos of Steinbeck were tacked up on the walls beneath stained glass windows. A black and white photo of JFK, exemplar of Camelot, hung on another wall.

Our oldest son stuck his head in the door and Richard executed another opulent welcome.

"John Steinbeck welcomes you!" He guided my son to sit next to me. "Welcome Paul," I seconded. "What the hell?" Paul whispered.

It was our youngest son's turn. "Ah, another handsome boy. Perfect." So, there we were, lined up on sofa, slightly dazed, like some Three Stooges scene in which we'd just been bonked as we stepped innocently through the door.

Richard stood over us: "We almost have a quorum for the Knights of the Roundtable."

Quiet as a forest doe, my wife materialized: tall, long dark hair, early fifties, an artist, as beautiful as when we met almost three decades earlier. Richard took her in, spread his arms in welcome and in full tremolo shouted: "Guinevere!"

My wife chose not to take the last spot on the sofa. "I'm fine standing," she said a little too cheerfully from her position closer to the door than the rest of us.

For the next half-hour Richard orated the life, works and times of John Steinbeck. Sometimes he brooded, head down, like Hamlet; other times he burst out with Falstaffian gusto. He whispered, he soared, he paced and pivoted as he unfurled a long and winding narrative, often connecting the author to the Arthurian heroic quest.

I thought of Chautauqua, of William Jennings Bryan, of the American revivalist tradition.

Richard said he had traveled around the country speaking about Steinbeck. I looked again at the blown-up photo of Richard with the smiling Bill Murray. From upstairs, at times, came a discreet thumping, which finally tapered into silence.

Richard passed around a first edition of "Grapes of Wrath." He held up old *Life* magazines containing pictures of Steinbeck. Eyes closed, he recited chunks of "East of Eden."

Once, in the heat of his performance, he teared up, then snapped back into his noble manner. The heroic quest, he said, was life's most worthy aim. He mentioned the young, unemployed scholar Joseph Campbell, future master of mythology, turning up in neighboring Monterey in his early years. Campbell, the equally unknown Steinbeck and Ricketts, whom Steinbeck met in 1930, held long discussion into the wee hours, Richard said. He quoted from Campbell's journal from those times: "John has a fine, deep, living quality about his work which ought to ring the bell, I think—if his work is ever discovered."

"Consider," Richard said, lowering his voice, "Heroes recognize heroes when no one else does."

Richard dove deeper into Camelot: The legend, which Steinbeck first discovered as a ten-year-old in the summer of 1912 through Thomas Malory's tales, absorbed the author all his life and resulted in his unfinished "The Acts of King Arthur and His Noble Knights," published posthumously in 1976.

Steinbeck's quest for integrity, keeping one's core intact, Richard insisted, was never more important in ourja age of greed and banality: "Living in our age is like being stoned to death with popcorn. Make no mistake, it will kill you."

Richard talked about the history of his cottage, and Steinbeck's maternal grandmother.

A gust of emotion swept the room when he brought up November 22, 1963 and how the shattering of JFK's skull shattered the dream of Camelot.

He mentioned the post-invasion mess in Iraq, then homed in on our two boys: "Don't let them go to this war." He looked at me, and then at my wife before he turned his blue-eyed gaze, like the swivel of a pair of long-range naval guns, to our boys: "Do Not Go!"

It was time for us to go. The curtain had come down. Richard signed our map: "To Nick & Paul, Great Luck with Your Personal Journey. John Steinbeck & Richard Andolsen." I gave Richard a firm handshake and a $50 bill. His profuse gratitude followed us to our car.

"I thought he was going to climb in and go home with us," I laughed as we headed for Monterey, and immediately regretted it. My wife and two boys were silent, still a little stunned. Finally, my wife said, quietly: "It's the best $50 you've ever spent."

Pacific Grove and Monterey touch each other in one of the most beautiful reaches on the central California coast. Monterey, population 28,000, is a pretty, historic city founded in 1770 with an old town. But Cannery Row is the main draw, especially in summers, with its restaurants, antique shops and high-end hotels. There's a Steinbeck wax museum, a couple of Steinbeck statues, a world-famous aquarium, tacky t-shirt shops and sidewalks jammed with ice cream cone lickers.

"They fish for tourists now, not pilchards, and that species they are not likely to wipe out," Steinbeck wrote about Cannery Row in "Travels with Charley," in 1962.

"Cannery Row," published in 1945, retails the shenanigans of Mack and the boys orbiting around the admirable Doc. It may be Steinbeck's most iconic work for many. Steinbeck said the book came because he was asked by GI's to write something "funny," something not about war.

For all of its status as a "fun" read, "Cannery Row" is Steinbeck's post-War book. He'd covered the European theater for the *New York Herald* and returned scarred. The short novel features two suicides in its early pages. Later, in a surreal scene, Doc happens upon a corpse of a beautiful young woman afloat in the tidepools of La Jolla: "The eyes were open and clear and the face was firm and the hair washed gently about her head."

Ed Ricketts, 1897-1948, was more than Steinbeck's friend, inspiration, incubator of ideas and owner of the Pacific Biological Laboratories, changed to Western Biological Laboratories in "Cannery Row." He was a respected marine biologist without a diploma, a deep ecological thinker and explorer of modern poetics who was ahead of his time. He was also author of "Between Pacific Tides," still an influential book, and at least part author, with Steinbeck, of "Sea of Cortez."

Ricketts' old lab at 800 Cannery Row is a low wooden building with a flight of stairs heading up to the former office and living quarters. He kept his specimens in the basement. Steinbeck spent two pages in "Cannery Row" describing in minute detail the jumble inside. Ricketts died in 1948 when his car collided with a train, the spot marked by a memorial bust in downtown Monterey at Drake Street.

All this is well known.

What is less known is the afterlife of 800 Cannery Row; how it evolved into the headquarters of a Monterey artistic circle in the 1950s. The Monterey Jazz Festival was conceived there. Famous guests visited: James Baldwin, Lenny Bruce, Earl Hines and a very frail Billie Holliday shortly before her death in 1959. The building was deeded to the City of Monterey in 1993. Free tours are now available with reservations.

An historically valuable book, "Doc's Lab: Myths and Legends of Cannery Row," by Ed Larsh, former basketball coach and English teacher at Monterey High School, published in 1997, captures the memories of the area's old timers—how it was when fishing and canning were king.

Three years after Rickett's death, Larsh entered Doc's lab with Harlan Watkins, the man who would rent it, and the lab's owner, Yock Yee of Wing Chong's grocery across the street—Lee Chong grocery in the novel. "It was as if Ed Ricketts had left the day before," Larsh wrote. "His record player, silent now, still held a Gregorian Chant."

Pacific Grove, "Butterfly Town, USA", population 15,600, is a lovely place of Victorian homes, craftsman cottages, Gothic and Pueblo revivals and a swimming cove at Lover's Point. The main village lies slightly inland, where the glow of marine light filters through the pine, cypress and eucalyptus trees. The Monarch butterflies return here in early fall.

Richard's cottage, now remodeled, stands at the western edge of town. His full name was Richard Martin Andolsen. Richard died on June 6, 2007 at age 79, according to a paid obituary in the *Monterey Herald*. The obit said he died peacefully "in the arms of his loving sister" at the local hospital.

Most likely the newspaper account of Richard's life was written by his sister.

He was born in Cleveland, Ohio in 1927, and entered the U.S. Navy at eighteen. After the Navy he attended Ohio State University where he played football and was a member of the wrestling team. He studied commercial art and worked as a publicity manager for venerable Loew's Stillman Theatre in Cleveland where he came into contact with a number of movie stars.

In his thirties Richard stowed away on the Queen Mary, jumped ship into "churning waters" and swam into Southampton, England. Arrested when he was found sleeping on a park bench, Richard's story "made headlines." He married a socialite, moved to southern California where he worked as a pharmaceutical salesman, moved on to Monterey, divorced, and opened an antique shop.

In his late sixties he bought the Hamilton cottage in Pacific Grove with his recently widowed mother. After her death, the house passed to Richard and his sister.

He founded the Steinbeck Arthurian Society and hosted numerous discussions at the cottage on his favorite subject. Along the way, Richard, "a maverick," according to the obituary, defended the changes he made to the house, despite building codes. "He was not a materialistic person, but he could fit into any class of society, not only because he was handsome and charming, but because of his brilliant mind."

Richard married again in the mid-1980s, traveled with his new wife, and made contact with Joseph Campbell and arranged for Campbell to speak in nearby Carmel, where he and others entertained the renowned mythology expert.

"Ever the promoter, Richard brought many famous people to his Steinbeck House and Museum hoping to pique their interest in the Steinbeck only he knew and understood." In the late 90s, Richard's only son was found dead in the house, "and thus began Richard's decline into depression and his hopelessness over the declining moral state of society."

Recently, I came across an item in the *Herald* published April 14, 2011, with this headline: "Pacific Grove Cottage where Steinbeck's grandmother lived being restored."

"A cottage that once housed the John Steinbeck Arthurian Spiritual Society Museum and where the famous author's grandmother lived is undergoing a major renovation," it begins. The article mentions the Steinbeck statue, built by "the late Richard Andolsen, founder of the museum," who acquired the house in 1960.

The current owner, the article went on, gave the statue to cartoonist Snick Farkas, "whose bi-monthly satirical 'Colossus of Gold' comic strip about city doings features the statue as the main character."

The article quotes Esther Trosow, who maintains a website about Steinbeck's connection to Pacific Grove. The statue was in Farkas' garage in pieces at the time. "It's unbelievable," Trosow said. "It was made of Bondo, plaster, chicken wire, newspaper, electrical wire, concrete. If they sell it in a hardware store, it's in that thing."

At the article's end a Carmel architect noted how the house "has been erratically altered over time." He continued: "To say the repairs and alterations on it were substandard would be polite. I would call it damaged."

All very, irresistibly droll.

In June 2008 Richard's cottage was put on the market with an asking price of $695,000—a low number reflecting the amount of work needed. This was a couple of months before the big crash. In January 2009 the cottage sold for $472,000. Today, according to Zillow, its value is listed at $1.2 million, though it's not for sale.

The widow's walk with the Pegasus weathervane has been removed.

In 1953 John Steinbeck wrote: "The western world and its so called culture have invented very few things...But there is one thing we invented...and that is gallantry...It means that a person, all alone, will take on odds that by their very nature are insurmountable...And also this same gallantry gives a dignity to the individual that nothing else ever has."

Near the end of Richard's obituary there's this: "On January 1, 2007, he was rushed to Community Hospital by ambulance. It has been reported that his cherished home and small museum were in terrible disarray, but the bed he was found in was piled with his beloved books."

And so, hardly noticed, another chapter closed on John Steinbeck's connection to the Monterey Peninsula.

"All great and precious things are lonely," Steinbeck wrote.

ANTHROPOETICS

"The revolution is to be human."
– Walter Lowenfels

Eric Greinke

The demographic movement toward an America wherein whites are no longer the majority is inevitable. Combined with the multiplication effect of the internet, the groundwork for a commonality-based poetics is steadily being established. It seems clear that there are several historically contemporary canons that run in parallel concurrence and seem to represent opposite poles of similar issues. By rising to a higher level of abstraction, these apparent opposites may be reconciled. I dream of a unified field where objectivity and subjectivity are expressed in greater balance for the good of all. It is a natural process that can bring us closer together and lead to artistic and humanitarian progress.

1. The Legacy of Ethnopoetics

In the late sixties and early seventies, Jerome Rothenberg and other theorists developed the ethnopoetic movement, which was a divergent response to the myopic dominance of white, upper-class, male, British and American poets. The ethnocentric seeds of the movement found fertile ground in neglected segments of the population. It is fair to say that the ethnopoetic movement led directly to the identity poetry of today. As an alternative route forward from the often-dogmatic modern poetry of Ivy League and Oxford poets, ethnopoetics was a breath of fresh air that stimulated diversity and creativity.

Among these, the emergence of Black poetry onto the zeitgeist had a profound effect on post-modern poetry and on social consciousness as well. Native American poetic tradition also came into the consciousness of poets, as well as greater appreciation of experimental European and South American movements (i.e. Surrealism) and giving contemporary voice to ancient Japanese forms such as haiku. From its ethnocentric roots, identity poetics eventually emerged.

Jerome Rothenberg's work in ethnopoetics blazed the trail for the current emphasis on divergent cultural positions such as racial, gender, and other identity groups. But he also has addressed what all these divergent positions have in common, and that's what I'm deeply interested in. Great truths seem to lie in paradox. Ethnopoetics has led us on two parallel paths which are likely to eventually converge. The identity poetics of the present zeitgeist can evolve into a poetry that emphasizes human commonality in the face of challenges to our entire species. Nothing escapes the yin-yang principle. Everything has an upside and a downside. An unforeseen negative effect of ethnopoetics is that it has led to ethnocentrism and cultural/social polarization. Ethnocentrism emphasizes our differences and finds its source of energy in that part of human nature that is selfish and competitive, when what we need right now, in this world of increasing conflict over dwindling resources, is an emphasis and understanding of what we have *in common*. We need to stimulate and express the *other* side of our nature, the altruistic and generous side. Human progress lies in this direction. Poetry can both reflect and promote our progress.

The inspiring performance of the twenty-two year old, Black, female poet Amanda Gorman at the inauguration of President Biden is a wonderful example of a poem that expressed the feelings of many people of all kinds at a time when we needed it.

The great value of ethnopoetics is the counter-balance it provides against elitism. Elitism and the dominance of W.A.S.P. poets was *bad for the art of poetry*. We would never want to go back to that restrictive time. Diversity is good for poetry, but so is seeing the big picture, where we have more in common than we are different, is a higher priority.

2. Universality

It would be good if more American poets had the intention of writing for the world. Universality is the primary value of all art. The current percentage of American poets who write for the international market is quite low. I guess it's maybe 5%. Poets need to develop the big picture and stop being so personally and culturally narcissistic.

Our greatest American poet addressed the issue one hundred and thirty-eight years ago:

> "Why not fix your verses henceforth to the gauge of the round globe? the whole race? Perhaps the most illustrious culmination of the modern may thus prove to be a signal growth of joyous, more exalted bards of adhesiveness, identically one in soul, but contributed by every nation, each after its distinctive kind. Let

us, audacious, start it. Let the diplomats, as ever, still deeply plan, seeking advantages, proposing treaties between governments, and to bind them, on paper: what I seek is different, simpler. I would inaugurate from America, for this purpose, new formulas—international poems."

– Walt Whitman
from *Poetry To-day in America*

Post-modern American poetry has attempted to break away from the "rules" of modernism, just as modernism itself attempted to deconstruct traditional conventions of the art. Unfortunately, post-modernism has now congealed into rigid conventions that inevitably choke and restrict poetry, an art that should always challenge conventional thinking. As such, it cannot remain static but must keep on moving like a Great White Shark. Different times call for different counter-measures against dogmatic thinking.

We American poets also need to address and understand our own national diversity. The best way to compare poets as seemingly diverse as Ginsberg and Angelou is on a higher level of abstraction, emphasizing their levels of passion, commitment, universality and morality.

We need to stop being distracted by surface elements such as form and style. The essence can be retained and developed while the surface qualities are transformative to various colloquialisms, forms and styles. While stylistic coloration may enhance (or distract from) a poem's foundation in meaning, it isn't the most essential component of a poem. Style is a relatively surface value that serves to *enhance* meaning. Meaning (or its implication) is a *fundamental* value of poetry.

3. Poetic Morality

The essential concept of poetic license means that every approach to and subject of poetry is legitimate art, but paradoxically, a moral hierarchy must necessarily exist because those poems that speak to and for the greatest number of people (in other words, the most universal), provide high-test fuel for human understanding, personal growth and social progress.

From a moral perspective, a poem's primary value is the degree to which it promotes mutual understanding and empathy. This may be conceptualized as a hierarchy of moral value. (I am not referring to prosaic moral proselytizing here, but rather to the evocation of common symbols and the universal myths that go with them.)

The first stanzas of *A Brave And Startling Truth* by the late Maya Angelou, illustrates the point:

> We, this people, on a small and lonely planet
> Traveling through casual space
> Past aloof stars, across the way of indifferent suns
> To a destination where all signs tell us
> It is possible and imperative that we learn
> A brave and startling truth
>
> And when we come to it
> To the day of peacemaking
> When we release our fingers
> From fists of hostility
> And allow the pure air to cool our palms
>
> When we come to it
> When the curtain falls on the minstrel show of hate
> And faces sooted with scorn are scrubbed clean
> When battlefields and coliseum
> No longer rake our unique and particular sons and daughters
> Up with the bruised and bloody grass
> To lie in identical plots in foreign soil
>
> When the rapacious storming of the churches
> The screaming racket in the temples have ceased
> When the pennants are waving gaily
> When the banners of the world tremble
> Stoutly in the good, clean breeze
>
> When we come to it
> When we let the rifles fall from our shoulders
> And children dress their dolls in flags of truce
>
> When land mines of death have been removed
> And the aged can walk into evenings of peace
> When religious ritual is not perfumed
> By the incense of burning flesh

> And childhood dreams are not kicked awake
> By nightmares of abuse

Poetry with high universal value transcends cultural limitations and ethnocentric concerns and speaks directly to the human condition. Poetry with medium universal value eliminates personal pronouns and restricts itself to imagery and description, achieving meaning through symbolism and/ or juxtaposition of images. Poems of low universal value address only the isolated personal concerns of the poet. Confessional or autobiographical poetry can also be in the other two, higher categories.

It would be unnecessarily difficult for any poet to restrict himself to writing all his poems in the high universal mode. Instead, each of us has a quotient of the percentage of our poems in both the microcosm and macrocosm.

Poems of relatively low universal value still have a poetic impulse behind them and they still need to be written even if all they accomplish is personal catharsis or identity with a group. Indeed, the majority of poets will continue to write at all three levels, but the focus has been too great on the lower type of poem. This may explain why poetry is seen by so many as useless and self-indulgent. But poetry has survived because it has *survival value* for our species, if only we can harness its power to open minds and hearts toward greater empathy and altruism.

4. Finding the Macrocosm

The concepts of microcosm and macrocosm are essential concepts in understanding universality. The universal unconscious and what we've come to regard as Jungian archetypes, is also an essential concept. According to Jung, the collective unconscious is a psychological inheritance. It contains all of the knowledge and experiences we share as a species as well as our personal versions of the universal archetypes. If each of us is a microcosm of "human," then one might assume that introspection by individuals (poets, etc.) will get us to the level of common human experience. It isn't that simple. In Jungian psychology, the archetypes represent universal patterns and images that are part of the collective unconscious. We inherit these archetypes much the way we inherit instinctive patterns of behavior. These archaic and mythic characters that make up the archetypes reside with all people from all over the world, and they symbolize basic human motivations, values, and personalities.

According to Jung, there are four primary archetypes (The Mother, The Father, The Shadow, The Anima/Animus). It's important to note that archetypes are not culture-bound. Every human has a Father and a Mother. We each have a part of us (Anima or Animus) that identifies with the opposite gender. We each have a dark side (The Shadow). There are also the many secondary archetypes which every human holds in common, yet with personal experience factored in.

A well-known example of the exploration and evocation of the Mother archetype is *Kaddish* by Allen Ginsberg. It is generally considered Ginsberg's greatest poem, more personal than *Howl*, yet also more *universal*, because we all must strive to understand and accept our mothers. *Kaddish* is a masterpiece on several levels. It is a perfect example of how an essentially confessional approach may function to represent a common concern. Beyond that, its subjects are love and death, the two great subjects that bypass all cultural limits and get right at the core of the human condition. At his best, Allen Ginsberg was a universal poet in the Whitmanic tradition.

Kaddish is cathartic for both poet and reader because it addresses particulars that also represent commonalities. A reader finds himself thinking about his own mother, mothers in general, the bond between generations and the nature of death itself, all evoking strong emotional responses. Here's an excerpt:

> O Russian faced, woman on the grass, your long black hair is crowned with flowers, the mandolin is on your knees–
> Communist beauty, sit here married in the summer among daisies, promised happiness at hand–
> holy mother, now you smile on your love, your world is born anew, children run naked in the field spotted with dandelions,
> they eat in the plum tree grove at the end of the meadow and find a cabin where a white-haired negro teaches the mystery of his rainbarrel–
> blessed daughter come to America, I long to hear your voice again, remembering your mother's music, in the Song of the Natural Front–
> O glorious muse that bore me from the womb, gave suck first mystic life & taught me talk and music, from whose pained head I first took Vision–

Tortured and beaten in the skull–What mad hallucinations of the damned that drive me out of my own skull to seek Eternity till I find Peace for Thee, O Poetry—and for all humankind call on the Origin

Death which is the mother of the universe!—Now wear your nakedness forever, white flowers in your hair, your marriage sealed behind the sky—no revolution might destroy that maidenhood—

The primary archetype of The Shadow is probably the archetype that has been explored and expressed the most. In fiction and drama, the antagonist (a.k.a. "bad guy") is ubiquitous because they would lack aesthetic tension without him. Humans are fascinated with evil, because each of us has a dark side. It is evident that readers and viewers do not identify exclusively with the protagonist/good guy. People wonder what evil they may be capable of given the right circumstances. Wherever there is personal or social conflict, The Shadow lurks.

As a species, we need to understand and address the war in man, the deeply-seated, built-in conflict that we homo sapiens have between the selfish, materialistic side and the altruistic, moralistic side of human nature. Our dual nature is the cause of most human crime, suffering and social conflict. The traditional symbols that represent our primate nature are an angel on one shoulder and a devil on the other. The angel represents the empathic, altruistic, aesthetic side of our nature while the devil represents the selfish, competitive, materialistic side. This conflict is species-wide and goes way beyond cultural differences. A better understanding of our conflicted nature can be achieved through poetry.

The primary archetype of the Anima/Animus has seen a lot of serious play in recent decades, reflected in gender identity concerns and gender rights issues. The art and poetry of our time has explored these concerns more than in any previous era. Jung thought that recognition of his inner female would help a man integrate it into a more expansive ego. Like The Father and The Mother archetypes, the Anima/Animus is universal and not culture-bound. It is no coincidence that Walt Whitman and his pre-eminent post-modern successor Allen Ginsberg made gender expression and exploration a major theme in their work.

The anthropological evidence supporting the existence of the universal unconscious is overwhelming. Symbols of the archetypes abound in every culture and every world religion. Ancient mythology from every part of the globe is remarkably similar, with minor differences being mostly semantic. Thus, the archetype of The Mother is represented in ancient Hindu by Shakti, Mother of the Universe. Roman Catholics have the Virgin Mary. In Greek mythology, The Mother is called Gaea, Mother Goddess. In Roman mythology, she's Juno, Queen of the Gods. In Norse mythology, she becomes Freya.

There is a long list of secondary archetypes (i.e. The Wise Old Man, The Hero, The Trickster, etc.) that appear in world literature, folk tales, myths and religions in endless variations. Homer's *Odyssey* explores the archetype of The Hero. Gandalf in *Lord of the Rings* is The Wise Old Man. American Indians symbolized The Trickster in the form of Coyote, whereas for the Vikings, The Trickster was Loki.

The archetypes reveal themselves through symbolism, which means that they also appear in our dreams. All humans dream, cultural differences notwithstanding. This is why surrealism stresses the value of dreams and dream symbols. In surrealistic art (including poetry) the goal is to explore and reveal a deeper reality. The word "surreal" literally means "super-real." Popular anthropological writers like Joseph Campbell have done a good job explicating these universal connections. The study of comparative religions also validates the prevalence of the archetypes in every human culture throughout history.

The relationship between symbolism and intentionality is generally misunderstood. In pre-modern art, symbols were consciously manipulated. *The Garden of Earthly Delights* by Hieronymus Bosch, is a good example. The large triptych is loaded with symbols that the people of the period recognized readily, but today these same symbols evoke a subconscious response similar to surrealist paintings. They are still powerful symbols, but their level of intentionality has been largely lost. Ironically, they may be more potent symbols when perceived subconsciously than they were when they were recognized and in general use. Symbols are implicit and built into the human psyche and do not require intention.

In addition to the universal archetypes, we have the elements and social problems in common. The elements (earth, air, fire and water) are similar to the archetypes, in that they are also universal. Climate change, tsunamis, earthquakes, massive storm systems, wildfires, floods, droughts, pollution of the ocean and atmosphere, extinction of animal species, etc. are all issues of concern to our entire species. Social problems such as drug addiction, poverty, human trafficking, terrorism and public health bypass all national borders and should be of concern to us all. If the worldwide pandemic has taught us anything, it is that we are all in this world together.

Poetry can address these critical problems. The archetype of The Shadow appears in every social problem, in the form of greed, hostility, brutality, and apathy toward others who suffer.

A poet's ability to access the macrocosm and relate on a common, universal level can be improved through divergent thinking, which exercises the mind to be more flexible. Looking beyond one's own borders opens an artist to the macrocosm. Reading and writing outside one's comfort zone is a good first step toward a vision of the Big Picture. Expansion of the ego is the goal. The art that results from a wider world-view may have enormous value as an instrument of world peace.

Having an attitude that is open to the possibility of writing a poem that expresses universal truth for the whole species is essential. Nurturing tolerance, divergent thinking and altruism in oneself prepares fertile ground for the seeds of inspiration. The connection is already there. We just need to see it.

5. Barriers

There are several barriers to the development of an Anthropoetic movement, but most of them aren't physical. With the development of the worldwide web, the potential for such a movement is physically doable, no longer prevented by geography.

A major factor in favor of the movement is the nearly universal acceptance of English as a second language. International anthologies in English are now the standard, and sell considerably better than anthologies in any other language. Based on the locater on my website, the vast majority of my own readers are international, with large readerships in China, India, Indonesia and the Ukraine.

No, the barriers are no longer primarily physical, but they are very real nonetheless. What these barriers have in common is that they are *mainly mental* on the microcosmic level and *social* on the macrocosmic level.

Ego-psychology provides us with an explanation of the phenomena with its concept of ego-boundaries. When an individual's ego development is poor, his ego-boundaries are restricted so that he identifies with only himself. As a person becomes more secure and self-actualized (another Jungian concept), he increasingly identifies with things and people outside himself. Great humanitarians (i.e. Mahatma Gandhi, Albert Schweitzer and Mother Theresa) have such widely expansive ego-boundaries that they strongly identify with all of humanity. Such a person may feel at one with the world. Quite simply put, if we all felt that way, we'd eliminate human suffering and war.

The mental barrier that keeps us from identifying with our fellow humans across the planet is primarily *selfish fear and envy* of those who are superficially different from ourselves. The differences we perceive as so immense and divisive are truly only on the surface, since we have so much more in common than we don't, yet they are so deeply felt that most of them have been institutionalized nationally and introjected personally.

Competition between nations over scarce resources promotes international conflict and economic subjugation of underdeveloped countries. Poetry cannot, by itself, solve these problems, but it can make us more tolerant of our differences and cognizant of our shared, basic human nature. Poetry can deal with abstractions that are not materialistically or nationally based. Improved mutual understanding is the basis we need for a more equitable sharing of basic material resources. As a species, we need to walk a mile in each other's moccasins.

Nevertheless, the problem for the individual poet is getting in touch with his humanity and composing his poems from that mental/emotional space. It's not easy to attain or sustain. We come, full-circle, back to ego-development. A poet who writes for catharsis or to resolve personal emotional conflicts might not *represent* as well as one who has matured beyond an adolescent state of mind. The narcissistic element contradicts universality. It is evident that over the long-term evolution of our species we have moved in the general direction of greater recognition of our common humanity, but it's been a slow struggle out of barbaric ego as we've each attempted to deal with the battles between the angels and devils that occupy our human shoulders.

Ironically, the greatest barrier to identification and empathy between individuals may be the increasing popularity of identity poetics, seen as an end in itself instead of as a step along the path to a more expansive ego-state for the poets, other artists and ultimately for the masses. The greatest instrument of anthropoetics may be that angel on one shoulder who coaxes us to walk a mile in other people's moccasins.

Material inequities have given the shoulder-devil his power. But the angel draws power from the human heart, from our capacity for love. We are not quite there yet, but we have always been headed in that direction because it is a natural evolutionary process. Evolution is based on survival of the species.

The arts both reflect and solidify our finest impulses, and poetry, because it uses words as its medium, can function as an instrument of human progress. This flies in the face of those who nihilistically claim that it has no real value or purpose. As Walter Lowenfels stated, so simply and elegantly: "The revolution is to be human."

Sources

A Brave And Startling Truth; Maya Angelou; Random House, 1961

Selected Poems 1947-1995; Allen Ginsberg; HarperCollins, 1996

The Revolution Is To Be Human; Walter Lowenfels; International Publishers, 1973

CANARY

Nikki Williams

The boy grips his prize, spurns the MC's embrace before well-dressed folks at the function. The eyes of one stoic face are trained on the pupil, tracing his timorous air. Rooting around without looking, the woman gingerly brings out butterscotch, gum, mints.

She is a bit too pleased when she offers to Dr. & Mrs. in her row.

She has already reneged when she leans over, leers at both.

Hot under the collar, she resumes her probe in padded silence.

She scrabbles at their stony hue, the boy's profile, the candy, tucks them tightly into her yellow clutch. They fold like fingers into the pouch, swallowed below its kiss-lock depths. Her knick-knacks secured, she tinkers with the embellishments a bit—its chain straps, zigzag fringe. She who slipped on life's lemons like a shawl, she whose heart of glass pumps gall.

She'll pore over the stash for many hours, nitpicking, pouring into any ear.

A spinster darning fables, a prick fabricating lives. Sizing up the shy boy in her trap, grafting away with restless shears.

Hurling hot air, she will rake mother, grandfather, ghosts over coals.

Singing like a canary stuck on a sour note; chucked like magic beans from the garden of credence.

HOLLYWOOD MOVIE

Karen Greenbaum-Maya

We expect a new day dawning at the end of a Hollywood movie. Doors opening to the new house, corner office with a window, a seat at the table, new love finally eager, Redford and Hoffman in the newsroom typing, old-school clackity-clack, while Walter Cronkite reads Nixon's crimes and downfall. The rejected girl revealed as hot without her glasses, powerful as Clark Kent in waiting. Now she's prom queen, now she realizes the worth of the decent nerdy guy, writer's proxy. We demand redemption or rebirth or total old world destruction. And it's gotta hit all the beats of the classic oldies sound track. The woman who finds new life and new love when her husband dies and sets her free, when she travels to Italy, when she tiptoes into Venice at last.

That same woman just blew through a red light. Didn't even see it, what with the movie playing on a loop in her head. The new road was a new experience but did not offer a new life. And she rear-ended a car when she dozed off. Heavy holiday traffic but she'd driven out to spend the night with the kids instead of waking alone, not to mention cooking the whole damned meal, the way she had for all those years. No, a different exhaustion, something new for a new part of life. She had no warning, no sense of drifting, just slipped into sleep, foot slipping off the brake and wham there she was.

Hollywood movies admit no half-measures. Nobody talks about the sound cutting out, the light bulb simply going dark without drama. Not even a crack or a flash. We want to hear the voice return, we want at least the bulb replaced so we can witness, be part of the story. Seriously, leaving the old life behind? Only in the movies. We can drive off the cliff, but we know it's a Hollywood movie when we see only the slo-mo launch of the convertible, not the landing in flames.

She watched her husband make his road trip. How other cars kept startling him, showing up out of nowhere right under his elbow when he needed to change lanes. Bit by bit she drove more and more, dreading the time when they'd have to have that conversation. Yet she hadn't really understood. The problem wasn't loss of powers, not even new limitations, not how he lost his way in the town where he'd lived forty years, not how he used to read the news in three languages and now couldn't follow the plot of a Hollywood movie. The problem was that never again would there be anything new. Casually he'd been stripped of every power that used to shine, ready as striking a match. He'd burnt-out, the way celluloid film melts and burns when the reels stop turning.

EIFFEL TOWER

Karen Greenbaum-Maya

The experienced tourist wants to get lost in Paris. It's not easy. The Eiffel Tower always shows up unexpectedly, sticking out from chestnut trees, floating over McDonald's golden arches, thrusting like a glimpse of a woman's haunch between Belle Époque buildings. The experienced tourist plays at getting lost. She sits down at the next random café and looks around for a hotel and a bakery. She could live out her life on this dowdy stone street. She could take up a new life in a tiny corner studio shaped like the Eiffel Tower on the next street that fans out from one of those étoiles where identical streets splinter off like the quarks from a split atom. She'll walk one more street and find herself standing across from her apartment, obvious as the Eiffel Tower. One day she bought sheets printed with the Eiffel Tower. She almost got lost in the Ste-Pierre, looking for Sacre Cœur, but when she came out of the shop, there it was, rising up on the hill like the sugar-cube model she'd made in 7th grade history.

The experienced tourist is tired of always knowing the way to the Eiffel Tower, such a sneaky structure. It looms silently through the milky air. No part of the Eiffel Tower could ever be part of anything else. The experienced tourist tries to confuse herself by turning corners every time she spots the Eiffel Tower. Nothing helps. The experienced tourist is tired of knowing the streets, of having a map in her head with all the monuments marked. She is tired. She is looking for a place so ordinary that she could never find her way home, not ever again.

MALL NIGHT, 2008

Natalie Gerich Brabson

A new post pops up on Elijah's Facebook wall. *Shoutout to Jackson FuturePilot Brown for giving me a break from this AP Chem hw. Movie, arcade, cheesecake for dinner, peace.* "Jackson FuturePilot Brown" is Elijah's cousin. Two months ago, Elijah would have made these same plans with me.

I write on my own wall, *Mall night!* Elijah and I are still Facebook friends. He will see this, text me, ask to meet up. I open Facebook in two tabs—my wall and his—and refresh both. Occasionally we still talk, on days I wait for him after his track practice.

Mom gets home a little after 7. I can see she's exhausted, but I ask anyhow if she'll drive me to the mall, knowing she'll agree.

In the mall, each store I walk past blares pop music, and my own footsteps are loud on the hyper-polyurethaned floors. Over everything, I listen closely for his voice, my name. I tuck my hand inside my purse and hold my phone there, waiting for the little buzz. He'll text, *Wanna meet up?* Or, *You at the food court rn?*

He doesn't. It's early enough, and he might still be watching the movie. I duck behind a kiosk selling a knockoff version of Obama's "Hope" poster, and after checking both ways to make sure I am not seen, I dip into Sephora.

There are throngs of people inside. They're hard to push past. Everyone seems to be stuck by a particular set of products, unable to decide what will help fix them.

When I'm far enough back to not be visible from the window, I look for help. There are several enthusiastic reps visible among the crowd in black-shirt/party-makeup uniforms, all trying to meet my gaze. I head toward the one rep who isn't already giving me a wide, open-mouth smile.

"What kind of event do you need a demo look for?" His nametag says Kenny. He's not wearing as much makeup as the other reps, only something shimmery on his skin.

I lie. "Prom. But not a fancy prom."

Kenny laughs. "Not a fancy prom. What kind of prom is that?" He begins blotting my face to soak up the oil. I close my eyes and pretend I'm not embarrassed. "That's the theme this year."

Kenny asks, "What's your dress like?"

"I haven't decided, maybe black." I feel guilty now for lying, and to avoid further prom questions, add, "I just want simple makeup. Something pretty but natural." When I walk around the mall later, when Elijah sees me, I don't want him to notice the difference—not consciously.

Kenny preps the station, and I hold my left hand in my right, imagining one of my hands is not my own. The station-prepping takes longer than I expect. I fiddle with and then flip open my phone. A yellow screen—there's a new text, and I hover my fingers over the QWERTY keyboard to respond. But it's not Elijah, not even my mom. Just a monthly update informing me I only reached 10% of my texting limit.

Gently, Kenny holds my face in his hands, tilting my head left and right as he studies me. He holds up a few shades of powder to my cheek. Finally, he says, "This one. This will do the trick."

THE GREAT CASHEW BUTTER WARS OF 1978

Arthur Davis

I was a reporter at the *Gainesville Tribune Reader* back then.

Not like the hard-hitting investigative reporters you see on major TV networks covering an international crisis or a gangland crime scene, or standing over the remains of a horrific train wreck.

It was 1978. Lego people, Van Halen, Garfield, Reese's Pieces, Pop Culture and more exploded onto the national scene. It was a massive year for superhero movies to disco hits. We had the perfect balance of wealth, work, and happiness. The cost of a first-class stamp was $0.13.

This was the sixth newspaper in my thirty-one-year career, and in the early months, as always, I was eager to prove myself to my editor. The assignment was straightforward: cover the National Cashew Butter Convention that was in town.

What's new in cashew butter you ask? Who are the leading scientists, and were growers impacted by the ruthlessly increasing black market in jumbo cashews? Still, I suspected that my editor was already feeling sorry for me and thinking up ways to keep me on the payroll.

Nuts of every kind were a big deal in Georgia's fragile economy, so any hint of corruption was going to be met with a quick, though not necessarily just, response.

The cuffs on my standard blue dress shirt were frayed, exposing the white fabric underneath. I was almost making ends meet, so this assignment was important. It would give me an opportunity to start my life over again, something I recalled saying to myself several times in the past.

I was finishing up my third workshop of the morning. Two reporters and too many unticked and curious were there. Most looked as bored as I was as the room slowly overheated on an already suffocating hot July, Georgia afternoon.

The panelists were experts in the field, but if you squeezed your eyes tight a little, they looked more like suspects in a police lineup.

One reporter asked a few trivial, offhanded, questions before he unloaded with, "How many of the panelists of this workshop on 'Criminal Activity in The Black Market Cashew Trade' are, or were, on the payroll of some vast international nut cartel manipulating the commodity prices of raw cashews?"

That woke everyone in the room.

The five panelists were in a difficult position. Each was tethered to a lie detector that the convention recently required all panelists to agree to wear because of the notoriety of hijacked delivery trucks, the sudden disappearance of leading cashew trade reformers, and the recent cashew scandals exploding in South American countries.

"Not me," the first panelist offered, somewhat too quickly I thought.

"Not me," the second added.

"Not me," the third and fourth followed.

"I don't understand the question," the fifth, heavyset, balding character said, puffing confidently on his cigar.

The overhead electronic lie detector screen indicated that each response sent the fine ink pointer swinging erratically from side to side on the scroll paper. A faint alarm was heard in the back of the small room and echoed in the electronic control center in the bowels of the convention center. People started pelting the panelists with questions, accusations, and tomatoes.

"How much graft do you get each month, and is it paid in non-sequential, small denominations?" one asked.

"How long have you been on the take?" another yelled, angrily.

"Which one of you is the most corrupt?"

"I want a list of all the names of your conspirators by sundown or my newspaper will launch a full-scale probe and follow each of you to the ends of the earth to get the truth?" a hardened, female reporter demanded to know, throwing her soda can at the panelists.

"My kid is looking for a summer job. Any ideas?" another reporter asked.

The doors swung open and two security guards shackled the five screaming panelists and started to drag them out of the room when trade protestors, who had been filling the streets in front of the convention center barged in, overpowered the guards, and yelled, "Let's lynch the bastards."

The guards, already soaked in a fearful sweat, fled for their lives as onlookers from other workshops rushed in and picked up the chant, "Lynch the Cashew Crooks. Lynch the Cashew Crooks."

The panelists were punched and kicked to the ground as the room filled up with the curious and crazed.

I stood in the back, which itself was no longer a safe place to be.

Heavy ropes soon appeared, and the first of the five panels was quickly strung up over the wooden rafters of the old convention center. The second put up a bitter fight, screaming something about "I have a wife and three children. You can't do this to me."

The room settled down after that and the third and fourth went quietly. The fifth, the guy who was still smoking away on his cigar, insisted there were a few good puffs remaining, so the mob gave him a minute to finish before they strung him up.

"Finally, a crook with some style," someone yelled from the back of the room

* * *

"This is great stuff," my editor said, poring over my story the next day.

"Thanks, boss. All a matter of hard work."

"Impressive. How many workshops did you get to attend?"

"Three. It was exhausting."

"I can imagine. I hate workshops, especially in that stifling shithole of a convention hall."

"Thanks."

"We might even feature this. It's such a fine piece of investigative reporting."

"Hard work and patience, and being able to sniff out the stories no one else can."

"So, 'Cashew Butter Convention Crashes As Air Conditioning Fails, Leaving Scores Unconscious.'"

"I think that says it all."

"Great, Frank. Well done. Take tomorrow off. You deserve it."

AT THE DARK

William Burtch

He lived with his widowed mother until she met that coal truck on a two-lane highway that needed three. Never wed. The house loomed above a lush central Pennsylvania cow pasture. Chipped leaded paint, once white, and cancerous wood rot. Native steps of stone consumed by insatiable grasses and weeds.

Rent on the century old farmhouse noshed up most of the disability check from his government job, his last and final. Rods and screws cobbled and coaxed his spine. Grief, unresolved, and recollections from his Army stint dogged him like hell beasts. Intrusions that nourished a creeping paranoia.

From the mine-dark reaches of the basement his fourteen year old nephew, Will, nabbed a three foot black snake barehanded. Will was a few days into his summer visit from California. The writhing reptile had entered through one of the gaping cracks in the foundation. It now drew its labored breaths in a dry glass aquarium on the kitchen floor. Flat black eyes peered out, vacuous.

Will's solo trip was his mother's suggestion. The passing of years and the three thousand mile divide had muted her understanding, her grasp of the gravity of her brother's lonely plunge into madness. She fostered instead images of an uncle and nephew bonding over fishing and ball games on TV. They did fish. Late on a humid night in the Susquehanna River, near Harrisburg. Strewn boulders broke the currents like ghosts treading the water. Night crawlers in a milk carton bed. Sweet raw earth.

The next night uncle and nephew sat hunched at the dining room table. Solid oak accented with decades of cigarette burns. Will raked the playing cards into a pile. He shuffled them for another hand of blackjack while gleaning the blood tinged tells of his uncle's eyes. Festering wells that betrayed. Eyes that offered up for confession the hard drink careening through his veins.

Gun-cleaning solvent fermented in the dining room. Assorted shotguns and rifles were housed in a glassed case against the wall. Draped like a trapper's blanket in the ether of the room were tales of ice and rain and chill-to-the-bone cold. Deafening blasts that shocked dying autumns and winters past. Whitetail deer tracked, harvested, gutted and quartered. Then the ethereal summer silence, lush and still.

"You alright, Uncle Ted?" Will asked.

"Why's that?"

"Don't know. Don't seem yourself."

Will pictured the exploding thumb tacks that had been pushed into the fence post that day. Tacks struck at fifty yards through a scoped 5mm rifle. Blistered into sprays of black metal mist.

"Didn't miss a single tack today. Either of us. Great shooting." Will said.

"Can't *ever* miss."

"Don't think anybody is that good."

"Better be. That's when they get you."

Will looked his uncle. Tried to tease meaning from his face.

"We're all just fodder. Remember that one. We're just fodder for someone or something else," Uncle Ted slurred.

Will sat back in his chair.

"Once I told you maybe I had been a spider. In a prior life," Will said. "Remember that?"

"There are no prior lives or future lives." Uncle Ted snapped. "We go cold as a miner's ass. Pitch black for all of time. At the dark. Nothing. Thank the Lord."

"Nobody knows that for sure. I think your soul, it gets freed. Your heat. Maybe straight into something else. "

Uncle Ted shoved his cards away.

"What might you be, Uncle Ted? In another life."

"Probably a goddamn snake. No better off than that serpent you have in the fish tank."

"Most people are scared of snakes."

"Damn well should be. I'm possessed. Eden's snake."

"No you aren't Uncle Ted. You're just tired."

"Well look at me. Will you?"

"God won't give you more than you can handle," Will said.

"Shit. And what if it's not God giving the orders?" Uncle Ted said, his eyes wide.

"It's my fault. Been running you ragged since I've been here. Maybe I should go back home," Will offered.

Uncle Ted became quiet.

Will edged away from the table. He expected his uncle to summon him back. Clarify things.

The wall clock chimed two in the morning. Will took the first steps of the brittle stairs. He stopped part way to peer back at his uncle. At the odd smile colliding with the entirety of his face.

Will shut the door of his tiny guest room and slid into his cot. He settled his gaze upon the sliver of yellow light under the door.

* * *

The wooden screened door slammed shut.

"Uncle Ted, I'm back," Will called out the next morning. He lifted the lid of the aquarium on the kitchen floor and tossed a small frog inside.

"Who is that?" Uncle Ted bellowed. "Who in Christ?"

"Just me."

Flat footed in his chair amid a roiling specter of exhaled smoke Will found his Uncle Ted. Punk beer in a glass sat on the side table. Next to it a near empty bottle of bourbon. Uncle Ted drew on a cigarette, burnt to its filter.

Beside the bourbon rested his Colt .45, a surplus semi-automatic from his military service.

"Sit down," Uncle Ted commanded. "Right there."

Will obeyed, sagging into the sofa adjacent to Uncle Ted. Crazed crimson eyes assessed him.

"How am I supposed to know who you are? Tell me that goddamn much."

Uncle Ted picked up the weapon.

"You know who I am. It's just me."

"The hell I know. Breaking into my house. Why wouldn't I just shoot you dead right now?"

"Uncle Ted, you're scaring me."

Uncle Ted waved the Colt around as though a piñata spun about his head.

"I'm possessed," he growled.

"You just need some help, Uncle Ted."

"Yeah? You can just help yourself the hell out of my house is what you can do."

"But Uncle Ted..."

"Get out. God knows what I might do if you don't."

Uncle Ted lowered the gun toward the side table, looking at it as though it might leap from his grasp like a feral cat.

Still quaking, Will advanced on a path to the kitchen. The glass aquarium was as he had left it. The snake was breathing, its tongue slow and heavy. A bulge had emerged in its scaled side, roughly the size of the frog. Will sought to get a handle on the aquarium. His probing fingers discovered a ridge under each side at the top, just below the lid.

Humidity had swelled the oak screened door snug to its frame. With a curt tug it squealed. He paused.

Uncle Ted heard the door. His eyes rolled from the bottle to the handgun.

Will slipped outside, the door left ajar. The morning sun struck him in the face like an open palm. Collecting himself, he descended the rickety steps of the porch. Through the dense dew cloaked fescue, he crept toward the edge of the cornfield. Fish tank and reptilian cargo firm to his chest. He reached the edge of the wood lot.

Dead steel, icy to the touch, like his mother's skin under the coal truck.

Will pushed deeper into the trees. To the small clear creek. Native trout hid beneath its overhangs. Late summers, the creek became only a trickle in its veiny lower reaches.

Will rested upon its bank.

Immense rocks nudged the course of the creek to the wider waters, to currents that quenched the greater rivers. Upon reaching the oceans, the waters carrying the spark of life, the heat, would resume the trek again in the warm renewing rains of spring.

Always the raging. The imagery. Frenetic. Bastards.

The rock where Will often sat warmed him. Dappled morning sun shimmied through a gap in the towering trees. Upon this rock he thought of what had come and gone. Conflict. Constant as breath.

The cadence of an odd prayer. Confessions. The commands. Sir, yes, sir!

The snake at first adapted to the tank being turned on its side. The gentle lapping of the brook the lone sound. It then advanced toward the lambent opening, as if called to the surface of the rock mere inches from its nose. Its tongue devoured the morning air.

In a final elegant torsion of its full length the snake became one with the rock. The sun's heat, its energy, gulped throughout the snake's scales. Its head held just above the surface, eyes keen, tongue frenetic.

Will and the snake were motionless. They basked and they breathed as though air was precious. The earth's delicate linen. Will cupped his hands with the cool fertile water. It cascaded down his throat and over his cheeks onto his shirt.

The icy steel then like fire. Like red coals.

Hoisting the empty aquarium and its lid, he backtracked. He reached the field of feed corn plump with blackening silk. The dew had dried. His steps crackled in the fescue. Autumn would soon leer, sowing its solemn pauses. Sowing death.

Will wiped sweat from his brow. He shaded his eyes back to the rock by the brook. To a rock now bare but for the frolicking rays of the sun.

THE RESCUED

Terry Sanville

Sheryl woke to the low rumble of the midnight sea as it rolled up the beach at Haleiwa. She reached for Steve but found only an empty bed and remembered her husband had some kind of special combat training that night. A full moon cast its blue light through an open window of their shoreline bungalow. Palm trees rattled in the wind.

A wild cry sounded over the waves. Sheryl sat up. The cry repeated. She slipped from bed and stumbled to the window. The crescent-shaped strand stretched before her, its wet sand gleaming like polished chrome. In the middle of a mirror patch something tiny moved. It struggled on four legs up the slope, crying out. But after only a few steps, the next incoming wave engulfed it and dragged it backward toward the surf line. The cries grew louder as it fought against the ocean's grip.

Sheryl tore from the house in her nightgown and ran full tilt toward the animal. It had quieted after the last wave and had stopped battling the water. Before the next bank of white foam overcame it, Sheryl bent and snatched up the bedraggled beast. Clutching its quivering body to her chest, she ran back to the house, not stopping until she reached the kitchen and flicked on the lights. The tiny cat, not much more than a kitten, resumed its crying, its little mouth open, pink tongue trying to lick its tabby coat.

Sheryl turned on the gas oven and opened its door wide. She placed a dishtowel on the flat door and set the cat on it. With another towel she gently dried the sodden feline in the blast of warm air. The cat nuzzled her hand and purred.

"Where the hell did you come from?" Sheryl said as she continued to massage the kitty until it stopped shuddering. She set it down on the kitchen tiles and it rubbed against her ankles. Could someone have tossed it into the sea to drown? Back at her family home in rural Pennsylvania, the farmers would drown unwanted kittens in their stock ponds. But on Oahu she thought maybe the locals had more respect for life.

The cat yowled.

"I don't have any cat food. How about some warm milk?" she asked.

Sheryl couldn't understand its answer. But when she heated a pan full and set it on the floor, the tabby lapped it up. It followed her to the bedroom, climbed onto Sheryl's pillow, nestled in her hair, and after a time snored.

The next morning, Sheryl smiled when she found the feline lying on its back on her chest, paws in the air. She gave a heave of the covers that drew loud complaints. At the village market she bought a bag of dry food. Returning to the bungalow she discovered all the paperwork from her desk scattered on the floor and the cat wailing.

"What's going on here?" Steve asked as he pushed through the front screen, still wearing his Army jungle fatigues. The camouflage face paint made him look ghoulish.

"I found it last night in the surf."

"Huh. So . . . you gonna keep it?"

"Yeah, it likes me. Purrs every time I pet it."

"Huh."

"Do you want a late breakfast?" Sheryl asked.

"No, I ate at the officer's mess."

"There's plenty of hot water for a shower."

"Thanks." Steve stretched out on the sofa and closed his eyes. "You know I'm shipping out to Vietnam in three months and you're going home. What'll ya do with that cat?"

"I haven't thought that far ahead."

"Maybe you should. Some local might want to take it."

"Yeah, well some local might have thrown it in the ocean. I'm keeping it. I need a companion when I go painting. I think it's a boy cat."

"Yeah, it's definitely male."

"I'm calling him Purr Machine or PM for short."

"Got it. I'm off to the shower."

"I'll be out painting most of the day. Will you be here for dinner?"

"Yeah. I can barbeque some steaks."

"Sounds great. I'll make a salad and we have beer."

In the hot and heavy air Sheryl sat on the sofa and stared at the dark TV. Beads of sweat formed on her arms. After drying off, she slathered herself with Coppertone, packed her art bag and portable easel, stuffed PM in her satchel, and left Steve to his shower and nap.

PM sat quietly in her lap as she drove their clapped-out Ford Falcon along back roads, past cut fields, the air filled with the earthy sweet smell of burnt sugar cane. She'd arrived in Hawaii during winter, coming from her family's Pennsylvania farm where everything looked white, black and gray. But on Oahu, she got to use all the blues and greens on her watercolor palette. She'd never seen such intense GREEN! Even after being on-island for nine months she still marveled at the lush life colors.

Sheryl found a tree-shaded cove at a rocky point and set up her easel and paints. PM scouted the area, staying clear of the ocean, and returned to flop at her feet as she sat and painted the seascape. The cat laid its head on her shoe and fell asleep, grumbling in its dreams. She wondered about the future, how her life would play out with Steve and the military, and what to do about PM.

Steven had attended a mixer at Sheryl's art college in New York City near the end of 1963, on a weekend pass from the U.S. Military Academy at West Point. He seemed so sure of himself. For Steve, questions and answers came mostly in black and white. And if he didn't know the answer he'd say, "My superiors know. I trust them . . . they know more than I do."

Sheryl fell for him, attracted to his clear convictions since her own frenetic life seemed more like a series of overlain watercolor washes that sometimes turned muddy. His handsome features helped seal the deal and she loved sketching him. But Steve had already married the Army, and Sheryl had just begun to understand how that would control their lives: frequently changing duty stations, losing and gaining friends, struggling to live on a tight budget, long separations, parties at the Officers Club swapping stories with other wives about husbands, families and war. It seemed to Sheryl that there would always be a war.

Among the wives, status depended on their husband's rank: generals' wives deserved the most respect while second lieutenants' wives, like Sheryl, deserved mostly sympathy. At a Fourth of July party at the OC, she had told a group of women that Steve trained to become a forward observer for the artillery. They averted their eyes and murmured inane comments: "that's nice," "you should be proud," "better than being cooped up in an office." Only later did she learn from Millie, the sergeant's wife next door, that forward observers didn't survive long in Vietnam.

PM slept. The sun dropped toward the blue ocean. Sheryl studied her painting and smiled. She liked how loose and impressionistic it felt. It captured the drama of the surging sea against the determined coastline without tying itself to any particular map coordinates. *Yikes, map coordinates? I really am starting to think like an Army wife. But the others think my painting is just a nice hobby. Hobby? Screw them. Bunch of troglodytes.*

Frowning, she packed her gear, scooped up an almost comatose PM and returned to their bungalow, to eat steak, sip beer, watch TV, and make love with Steve as if it would be their last time together.

* * *

"So what do you think is wrong with him?" Sheryl asked the veterinarian.

Dr. Chén sighed. "I could do tests but I've seen this many times. Your cat has distemper. Not much hope. Only strong ones survive."

Two weeks after pulling PM from the surf, Sheryl had noticed him stumbling. His eyes wept as if from some allergy and he kept sneezing. Then the diarrhea hit and she found repulsive accidents throughout the house.

Steve had issued one of his unequivocal orders, "Get rid of that thing. It's disgusting."

Sheryl had refused, found a strong cardboard box, filled its bottom with beach sand, and had hurried off to the veterinary clinic in Honolulu.

Now, sitting in the examination room with the vet prodding and poking PM, her chest ached with the thought of losing her new companion. *Maybe this is some kind of training, a test. If I'm to stay with Steve and be a good Army wife I need to toughen up, get used to fear and death. But why should I?*

"Isn't there something you can do?" Sheryl asked. "There must be some medicine I can give him."

The vet smiled and rummaged in a cabinet. "Give it these pills twice a day. Even if the cat seems to get better, keep giving it the pills until they're gone."

"Anything else? There's gotta be more."

"It won't like taking the meds. Give it lots of water after you place the pill in its mouth . . . and feed it more water throughout the day. I'll give you a needleless syringe you can use."

"Is it safe for the cat to go outside?"

"Probably not. Keep it away from other cats, someplace warm with its litter box and food close by. Use bleach to keep the area clean."

"Do you want to see him again?"

"No need. If it gets better, you'll know. But . . . but the chances are slim."

On the ride home, Sheryl's mind reeled with what she must do: close off and scrub down the laundry room where the water heater's pilot light would keep PM warm at night; buy a litter box and litter; lay in a supply of food; and explain everything to Steve.

Sheryl pushed through their bungalow's screen door, the cat yowling in its improvised carrier.

"Why'd you bring it home?" Steve asked.

"The vet said he could survive distemper. Don't worry, I'll take care of him . . . keep him out of your way."

Steve shook his head slowly and continued reading the Stars and Stripes newspaper, muttering to himself. He grabbed his first beer of the day and retired to the lanai.

Sheryl purchased a pair of strong leather gloves and wore them whenever she handled PM. At first the cat struggled mightily, even in his weakened state. But as days passed, he grew to trust her, although she suspected that squirting water down his throat six times a day probably felt like torture.

Three weeks in, the diarrhea slowed then stopped. PM showed a renewed interest in food. By six weeks he had recovered enough that Sheryl again stuffed him into her satchel when she went painting. By two months, he'd fully recovered, except the virus seemed to have quelled his playfulness. He now loved lying in the sun and staring at the Pacific, as if daring it to try and snare him again. Otherwise he stayed close to Sheryl and would purr whenever she picked him up.

Steve's departure day arrived. His entire battalion boarded transports docked at Pearl and set sail for Vietnam, to establish the field artillery in the Đắk Tô Valley. Their last days together had been strained and he spent nights with his Army buddies at the Officers Club while PM sat on Sheryl's lap and she stared numbly at the TV. Neither she nor Steve talked about his not coming back from the war. But neither could she stand the false bravado that some of the Army wives displayed. She found no comfort there. They seemed alien, badly acting out roles, reading lines written by someone else.

"So, when you get there send me your address," Sheryl told Steve right before he climbed aboard the troop transport. "I'll write, I promise."

"You'd better. I'm sorry I haven't been good company."

"Me either . . . and I understand. I'd be drunk as a skunk if I were going off to war."

"Don't think that didn't cross my mind. But the year will go fast, so they say."

"I hope so. But stay . . . stay safe. Bring your love back to me."

"I will."

Except during the early days of their engagement, Steve never mentioned love, never talked about future plans, never showed much interest in her art. She attributed his coolness to his pending date with fate in those far-off jungles of South Vietnam. But she also had a nagging suspicion that maybe going to war would be a relief for him, fulfilling his own personal manifest destiny. And besides, why the hell would a career Army officer want to live with an unknown capricious artist who painted blobs of color that defied description?

She watched the troop transports depart Pearl Harbor and only left the docks when PM complained, cooped up in her satchel without food or litter box. During her last two weeks on Oahu she painted every day from dawn to dusk, trying to capture forever the wild feel of landscape, people, and villages so full of color and life.

* * *

Sheryl and PM departed Oahu on a Matson liner bound for San Francisco. Stuffing him into a cat carrier had been the greatest challenge. Neither of them wanted to leave the island.

They eventually arrived at her parents' farm in Pennsylvania the day after Thanksgiving. Her folks weren't real farmers; they leased their land and barns to Pennsylvania Dutchmen who planted grain crops and tended dairy cows. They had purchased the farm in the early 1950s and moved her father's freelance design business from New York City into the old stone farmhouse.

Snow stood knee high on the ground when Sheryl and PM arrived. She shivered uncontrollably, eyes crying from the cold and from the loss of island smells and colors. She hurried to her old upstairs bedroom and put on winter clothes, PM complaining all the while from inside his carrier. When she finally let him out, he shot downstairs. She caught up with him in the living room where he faced off her parents' two huge tomcats, PM's tail fluffed out, ears laid back, and a low rumble coming from his throat.

"Don't worry, honey," her mother, said "they'll get used to him soon enough. It's all about territory."

"I'm more worried about how he'll handle the snow."

Sheryl cleared a space on the enclosed back porch for PM's litter pan and food bowl. But he proved bolder than she ever expected. He secured the best warm spot near the fireplace, watched TV while resting on the back of the sofa near Sheryl's ear, and sidestepped the aggression of the two fat bullies. One morning she came downstairs and found lumps of fur scattered around the living room, and it wasn't from PM.

"What happened here?" Sheryl asked her mother.

"Your cat laid into Mr. Moto. I had to pull them apart." Her mother examined the angry red scratches on her forearms.

The giant Siamese sat in a wingback chair and glowered at the two women.

"I'm sorry," Sheryl said. "I've never seen PM fight."

"Well, you've got a tiger there. And he keeps dogging me every time I go near the door. I know he wants to get out."

"Yeah, I've seen that too."

Sheryl had retrieved her battered VW Beetle from the barn and ventured into the snowy Pennsylvania hill country, PM lying on a blanket next to her and staring at the whiteness flying by. She painted icy creeks, covered bridges, barns, skeletal oak and maple forests, Christmas scenes that she made into cards for her parents to send to friends and relatives. The side of her artist pallet that held all the shades of green paint dried and cracked. Only the red blaze of the eastern cardinal added color to her winter artwork.

On these painting trips, PM mostly slept in the car. The few times when he attempted to cross a snowfield he kept shaking himself every few steps, sinking over his head in the deep spots, and complaining all the way.

Over brandies one night, Sheryl and her father paged through the huge portfolio of artwork that she brought home from Hawaii.

"You need to add more edges," he complained. "And use something more than green. It feels like I'm staring at a salad."

"You should go to the islands, Pop. All us mainland artists have to learn to see differently. And it's more than just the colors that are different."

"You're probably right. But even Rousseau painted tigers and jungle scenes with lots of edges."

Sheryl grinned. "Yes, but he produced those paintings in his French studio; never left the country."

As winter gave way to spring and summer, Sheryl and PM enjoyed the Pennsylvania countryside more and more. But the greenness didn't satisfy her longing. She missed the roar and whisper of the sea, the scent of warm ocean breezes, the cry of gulls in the morning, the feel of beach sand under bare feet. She had been to the Atlantic before. It felt like a cold stormy lake put there for nautical commerce. But the vast blue-green Pacific . . .

Steve was due to return to the States during the first week in November. It snowed early that year and by Halloween the farm had already weathered two storms.

"What have you heard from Steve?" Sheryl's mother asked. "I know he hasn't been writing as much but he should be stateside soon."

Sheryl groaned to herself and tried to control her facial expressions. "Yeah, I got a letter from him last week. He got promoted to first lieutenant and got his new duty assignment. Be back for a thirty day leave."

"Well that should be nice for you kids. You haven't talked much about him lately."

"I know. I've been trying to remember our time on Oahu, but it's getting harder."

"You know, honey, you're gonna have to get used to this. You're married to an Army officer. Where are they sending him next?"

"He's being attached to an artillery battalion at Fort Sill, Oklahoma for 90-days TDY. Then they'll fly him to Korea for 18 months."

"Lord, that's quite a change," her mother said and then in a lowered voice, "Are you going with him? You know, you can always stay here until he gets a stateside assignment."

"Thanks, Mom. We haven't talked about it. I'm waiting until he gets here."

For the rest of the day Sheryl avoided her parents. She knew they loved Steve, felt his influence could moderate their daughter's sometimes-erratic behavior and drag her back from her deep depressions. But Oklahoma? Then Korea? Even less green anytime of the year.

That night at supper she drank more New York wine than normal. PM curled at her feet and slept fitfully, rousing himself every few minutes to trot to the kitchen door before returning. Sheryl excused herself and holed up in her room, lay on the bed and stared at the ceiling. She tried reading but it wouldn't calm her nerves. The cold autumn tugged at her spirits and she dreaded meeting up with her husband, fearing what she might say or do.

Over the TV's muttering, she heard her mother call, "Sheryl, come down here, quick."

She bolted from bed and hustled downstairs. Her mom stood in the kitchen, wringing her hands.

"I'm sorry. PM must have slipped past me when I opened the door to take out the trash. I've called to him but he won't come. Can't see a thing out there."

Sheryl ran upstairs and put on her snow boots, heavy wool jacket and gloves. She grabbed a flashlight from a kitchen drawer and headed outside.

"I'll be back when I find him," she told her mother.

"Be careful, honey. It's freezing and there's black ice on the roads. And stay clear of the farms. You'll raise a ruckus with the barn dogs."

Sheryl carefully descended the slippery back steps and stopped, played the flashlight beam over the snow. A faint trail of paw prints headed westward across the bottom field toward the far woods. A gibbous moon turned the snow bluish and the wind cut through her wool jacket like it wasn't there. She proceeded slowly, calling out to PM as she went. The snow crunched under her boots. She came to a barbed wire fence at the edge of their property. Cat prints continued across the Glatfelter's field, heading for the woods.

In the distance she heard a faint cry, reminding her of the night she had rescued PM from Oahu's surf. Her heart ached with the memory and she quickly ducked through the wire fence and hurried toward the sound, calling out every few steps. A chorus of dogs barked. She ran across the snowy field, blowing steam in the frigid night air and calling to PM, "I'm coming, kitty, I'm coming."

The cat tracks veered sharply uphill into a thicket of black oaks. She picked her way through the tangled trees, stumbled and fell onto the rock-hard ground but was drawn forward by PM's shrieks and the barking dogs. A tree branch raked her face and she cried out, pressed a gloved hand to her cheek and kept it there.

The beam from her flashlight dimmed. She came to a clearing, the cat's cry near. She approached a tall maple and stopped. Three dogs sat on their haunches, their wagging tails dusting the snow. They whined and looked upward. Sheryl pointed the meager light into the tree, its beam caught the eyes of PM, halfway up.

"Go home," she yelled and stamped the ground.

The dogs looked at her and cocked their heads as if to say "Really? We do all the work and now ya want *us* to leave?"

But with constant commands, the hounds finally turned tail and headed home.

"Come here, kitty, come on down," she coaxed.

PM backed down the tree trunk until she grasped him, his wet body shaking. She unbuttoned her jacket and stuffed him into the top and re-buttoned it. PM head-butted her chest and purred.

"So why the hell did you come out here? Were you running away? How many times do I have to do *this*? When is it my turn?"

As usual, Sheryl couldn't understand the cat's reply. By the time they reached the house, PM had fallen asleep, the rise and fall of his warm belly felt right as rain.

Her mother greeted her in the kitchen with a cup of hot chocolate. They placed PM on his favorite spot near the living room fireplace to steam dry. Her father glanced at them and smiled then returned to watching TV with Walter Cronkite and the Evening News – flashes of young soldiers jumping from hovering helicopters into an open field and taking fire from the Viet Cong. Anti-war protesters in San Francisco replaced the combat images. Sheryl shuddered.

Back in the kitchen, her mother asked, "What happened to your face?"

Sheryl touched her numb cheek. "A tree branch got me."

"Well you've bled a bit but it doesn't look deep. Might leave a scar."

"Yes, I'm sure this place will leave its mark."

"What's that supposed to mean?"

"Nothing, Mom. Nothing. I'm just tired."

She climbed the stairs and entered her room with PM at her heels. Lying on her bed, she trembled, pulled the quilted spread over her head and closed her eyes. PM mewed and she let him slide in next to her. From downstairs the TV continued its mutterings. Her parents talked and Sheryl felt sure that they talked about her. *I should get up and take off these clothes, clean my cheek, and maybe . . .* Exhausted, she scooched under the covers and with PM nestling in her hippie-length hair, fell asleep.

Morning broke bright and cold with frost feathers on the insides of the windows. Her mother brought her a cup of cocoa and a heated scone, a recent Sunday morning tradition.

"Your Father and I will be leaving for church. We'll be there until almost noon. Do you want to come?"

"No thanks, Mom. But thanks . . . for everything."

"You're welcome, honey." Her mother paused at the bedroom doorway, shook her head then left.

PM batted her face, wanting his morning food. She flung back the covers, undressed and took a quick shower. The scratch on her cheek looked ugly, but once cleaned up it lost its drama. She wondered if Steve would complain and those thoughts caused her heart to pound. She gritted her teeth and pulled on a clean set of winter clothes.

Her parents' station wagon rumbled down the long driveway to the County road, its tailpipe smoking. She fed PM then hauled her artist's gear to her car and stowed it in the back seat. From her closet she removed a suitcase and packed it full of clothes and personal things, leaving her framed wedding picture on the dresser. She hardly recognized the woman in the photograph.

Lastly, she stowed PM's cat carrier, food, and litter box in the trunk, braided her hair into two long pigtails, and wrapped a colorful scarf around her head and across her forehead. She looked like a ghostly Indian princess.

"Come on, PM, time to go," she murmured.

The cat tore downstairs and waited at the kitchen door. She scribbled a note on the back of an envelope and left it on the table next to her father's half-empty coffee cup. Checking her purse for cash and gasoline credit cards, she grabbed PM and hustled to her VW bug, placing the cat on his blanket.

The engine clattered to life. Sheryl adjusted the rear view, trying not to stare at the sober face looking back. She gunned the VW and muscled the tiny car down the rutted driveway, to the County road and the Interstate beyond, heading west. PM purred, his hind legs balanced on the edge of the seat, his front legs on the dashboard, staring intently through the windshield as the dull countryside flowed past. By dawn the next day they breathed in the cold dry air of the southwest desert. By sundown off the Santa Barbara coast, the green Pacific rolled before them and they slept that night under palms once again.

Author's Note:

Lots of things influenced my writing of *The Rescued:* my military service during the Vietnam War; the unreported experiences of military wives and dependents; and the struggle between the disciplined nature of Army life and the beauty- and drama-seeking temperament of creative people. Much like the cat in my story that was rescued from the sea, my artist protagonist must save herself from a life where she doesn't fit. I always wonder how many other people feel in need of rescue.

JASPER

Robert Boucheron

Tuesday morning, Louisa Abernethy Jones stood at the kitchen sink with a mug. She leaned forward and peered slantwise out the window. The back yards made up a collective garden. At winter's end, it was bleak—bare trees, stubble, and matted vines. Harold found the house on Sycamore Avenue soon after they were married.

"A dream house it ain't," he said, "but we can afford it."

"I love it," Louisa said.

At the northern edge of the historic district, the house was in walking distance of everything. Doggedly, the Joneses rescued the yard, repaired the house, and stretched their dollars. They raised two children, and they paid off the mortgage. Then, on the threshold of freedom and security, at age forty-nine, Harold was "thrown in the slammer." That was how he phrased it, lying on a gurney after his "cardiac arrest."

A radio burbled in the background, and the whoosh of a passing vehicle filtered in from the street. A snuffle and whine at her feet made Louisa look down. A small, black, wrinkled face looked up and implored. The face was attached to a fawn-colored body on four stubby legs, a miniature clown with a tightly curled tail, a pug.

"Jasper, do you want to go out?"

Jasper wriggled in an orgy of yes. He had been Harold's idea. The children wanted a dog, and Harold wanted one that was not too big. On a visit to the animal shelter, they found Jasper. A puppy, he was the runt of the litter, according to the shelter attendant, the last one left. Despite this pitiful tale, Louisa recoiled on first sight.

"He's not just another pretty face," Harold urged.

"He's so ugly, he's cute," Gwen said. As a teen, she was always in cahoots with her father, in a secret alliance against her mother. "You have to love the little guy."

The little guy had personality. Years later, Gwen was married and gone, Harold had cracked his last joke, and Jasper remained. Now he was getting old. Sneezes and snuffles grew desperate, and stubby legs moved stiffly. While Galahad was away at college, the dog attached himself to Louisa.

Galahad rarely appeared in the morning. He stayed up late, listened to music through earbuds, and surfed the internet. A young man with a degree in medieval studies would find jobs scarce in his chosen field at the best of times. Louisa hoped something would turn up. Common sense suggested it would have little to do with courtly love or the search for the Holy Grail.

Louisa drained her mug, rinsed it, and set it in the sink. She walked to the hall with Jasper hot on her heels, took his leash from the coat tree, and clipped it to his collar. She slipped on a coat, the old one she wore for walking the dog. She grasped the leash firmly in her left hand, pulled open the door with her right, and they set forth.

Jasper trotted ahead at the limit of the leash. Sycamore Avenue was fascinating. No matter how many times they went this way, there was something new to see and smell. At the house with the privet hedge, the dog became wary. As they approached the gap he balked. A big ginger cat lurked in the path to the front door. With its fur raised, the cat looked bigger than Jasper.

"It's only Iggy," Louisa said. Ignatius the cat was friendly enough with people but arrogant with animals. He knew Jasper, and he hissed.

"Ignore the silly cat." She walked briskly past the gap.

Jasper gathered courage, ran after Louisa, and in a moment he was busy again. They reached the corner of Main Street, and it was Louisa's turn to stop.

"Local Musician Slain," the *Vindicator* shrieked from its bright blue vending box. This was the story Mavis had phoned about. The newspaper was delivered to Louisa's house, rolled and thrown from a bicycle. She had read the story. But she felt compelled to stand on the sidewalk and peer through the grimy glass. Jasper whined.

"You're right, there's no point in reading it again. Let's cross the street after this car. Do you want to go as far as the creek?"

Jasper looked up and snuffled. His eyes bulged, bright with anticipation.

"All right, but if you get tired on the way back, don't expect me to pick you up like a baby and carry you."

Which is exactly what she did, of course.

*

The *Vindicator* occupied a storefront on Main Street, with creaky floorboards, a high ceiling of pressed tin, and a lingering odor of printer's ink. Walter Nickles, necktie loose and shirt rumpled, sprang from his disaster zone of a desk. He took Louisa's coat, tossed it over a chair, and offered her a cup of coffee.

"I made it myself," he said.

"That's what I'm afraid of."

"You got my phone message?"

"I did. 'Come into the office A. S. A. P. Have I got an assignment for you!'"

"Word for word."

"Mindless repetition is my hobby."

"Did you know Ralph Willis?"

"Not personally. I heard him play the organ. He gave a recital at St. Giles once a year."

"Never made it there myself. You can get to know him a whole lot better."

"How is that possible if he just died?"

"You can write a follow-up for next week."

"I have no training in journalism."

"I'll coach you."

"Jimmy Kidd is your reporter. I'm an ordinary, middle-aged woman who has her hair done on Thursday and plays bridge with the girls on Friday."

"By the way, your hair looks stunning." Nickles smiled ingratiatingly. "People still play bridge?"

"Yes, we do. The same deck of cards you play poker with."

"Then why so standoffish?"

"When Ruth Garrison retired, you asked me to take over the lifestyle column, Tittle-Tattle. I learned on the job, and now everyone seems to enjoy reading my pieces. They're light, not too filling . . . like whipped cream. I'm not sure I can handle a police story, a grisly shooting."

"No, no, no! I want an in-depth profile, a human interest story. A tribute to the late artist, the man and his music, something like that. Talk to people who knew him, dig into his past, tell us why we should remember him fondly."

"Interview friends and family?"

"You have a knack for it."

"I don't know."

"This is right up your alley."

"What if I uncover something . . . unpleasant?"

"If it's shocking or sensational, so much the better."

"What if people prefer not to talk?"

"Exert your powers of persuasion, your special gift."

"I have no special gift."

"Don't sell yourself short, Louisa. You're a fine figure of a woman with a keen eye, a level head, and a nose for news. In your capable hands, Tittle-Tattle went from tedious social notes and stray gossip to . . . whipped cream! Now, if you're too busy with household chores and picking the lint from the dryer vent . . ."

"If anything, I have too much free time."

"And you're ready to sink your claws into something."

"This story may be too big for my delicate touch."

"Scared to learn a new skill?"

"I'm trying to be realistic."

"How do you see the story? Walk me through it."

"Ralph Willis drops dead in his own house. Nobody had a reason to shoot him that we know of. He was a church musician, not a drug lord or a stool pigeon, something that gets a person bumped off." Louisa made a helpless gesture.

"Accidents happen. The police think it was bad luck."

"What do you think, Walter?"

"I think you are ideally qualified to sniff out the truth."

"How will I know the truth when I find it?"

"We'll work on this together, your instinct and my expertise."

"Assuming we dig up something, what good will it do?"

"How will it help Willis? It won't. But I have a hunch certain people know more than they're letting on. The police are dragging their feet. Are they understaffed, not very bright, or just plain stubborn?"

"Do you want me to butt heads with Captain Ryder?"

"Wheedle him. Insinuate your way into his heart. See if he has a soft spot, an interest in bird-watching, a secret talent for watercolors."

"And if he has none?"

"The head-butting may come later. Leave that to me."

"Is this an in-depth profile or an investigative report?"

"Make of it what you will."

"Do I get paid?"

"Not only do you get money, you get glory—a byline. Will you give it a shot?"

"I'll give it a try. Let's watch our metaphors."

"Good. If you're correcting my metaphors, then you're already on the story."

"And this is a church-related matter. People are sensitive."

"All the more reason for a blasphemer like me to stay in the background."

"You don't swear."

"I can if provoked. Want to hear a sample?"

"Another time." Louisa reached for her coat. "Right now, I want hear what Captain Ryder has to say."

*

When Louisa got home, the sun had set. The house on Sycamore Avenue looked gloomy in the gathering dusk. She flicked the light switch in the hall, and a lamp emitted a feeble glow. After the color and sparkle of the Wolfram interior, not to mention the all-white kitchen Flibbert was installing, her domicile looked dim.

From the living room came an explosion of sneezes and snuffles. Jasper scurried into the hall as fast as his legs would carry him. Louisa peered down at the black, wrinkled face and large eyes.

"Poor Jasper! Did you miss me?" She bent to pet him, and the effort reminded her of how tired she was. "I suppose you want to go for a walk after being left in the house all day."

Jasper wriggled in the affirmative.

"Did Galahad go out, too? Were you all alone on guard duty? If you can wait a minute, we'll trot around the block. Then it will be time for you know what." She withheld the word "dinner" to forestall an outbreak of whining.

Louisa hung her coat on the tree and walked to the kitchen. Her mug was still in the sink where she left it that morning. A plate and glass had joined it, both dirty. Galahad had eaten lunch, which in his case was breakfast. Louisa reached for a clean glass, filled it with water from the tap, and drank it. After the unaccustomed cocktail, she felt parched.

A disheveled young man in socks shuffled into the kitchen.

"Hi, Mom."

"Good morning and good evening to you."

"What's for dinner?"

"I've had a long day, and I just this minute stepped in the door. Whatever is in the fridge is what's on the menu." She paused and glared at her son.

"You were gone all day?" He smiled sheepishly.

"Honestly, Galahad, sometimes you make me wonder. I have been interviewing people for an article. I walked all over town, asked pertinent questions, got evasive answers, and now I'm dead on my feet and ready to scream. Meanwhile, you lounge about the house, never lift a finger, and ignore Jasper, who is panting in distress."

"Sorry. I was reading Old French and surfing academic websites for job listings. I forgot about Jasper. When you're not here, he dozes on the sofa."

"If you made an appearance before noon, I could tell you what I am doing. Do you expect me to write you a letter?"

"No."

"And you can at least clean up after yourself."

"You don't like people in your space. Remember that sign you had? My Kitchen: Trespassers Will Be Boiled in Oil. What article?"

"The editor asked for a long piece on Ralph Willis, the man who was killed. Surely, you saw the news."

"Today's newspaper? I saw the front page. But you write that social column, and you don't have to meet a deadline."

"This is different. I suppose it's journalism."

"How long will it take? Will you be working on it full time?"

"I don't know. At this rate, it will keep me running around for days. I don't even know what the story is, how it will turn out. The police have no idea who shot Willis, and it is not at all clear that anyone cares."

"You do."

This remark caught Louisa short.

"Did you know Ralph Willis?" he asked.

"Only by reputation."

"If it involves so much effort, why did you take the assignment?"

"Walter Nickles talked me into it."

"Mom, do you expect me to believe that?"

"Willis's death strikes me as wrong. It's more than a mystery or an unsolved crime. It's a slap in the face to all of us. Or to those of us who think and act like responsible adults."

"I'm a responsible adult," Galahad said. "If you grant kitchen privileges, I won't break things."

"I will think about it. For starters, you can take poor Jasper for a walk." She glanced down at Galahad's feet. "After you put on some shoes."

"Okay. Did you hear that, poor Jasper?"

Positive body language.

"Meanwhile, I am going to *take off* my shoes and soak my feet in Epsom salt."

As Galahad and Jasper scurried away, Louisa sank into a kitchen chair. What a relief to sit and do nothing! It felt good to be home, be it ever so humble.

*

The next two days were busy. A weekly appointment at the beauty shop should have been a reprieve, but wasn't. Louisa walked home in a reflective mood. Her recent activity was a topic around town. People saw it as prying. Joe Flibbert hinted that he knew more than he was willing to tell about Ralph's friends. Eric and Blair Wolfram showed the limits of neighborly concern. Laetitia Tharpe was coolly detached from a man who was her former student, who lived on the same street, and who led her in the choir twice a week, at rehearsal and on Sunday morning. Is that what happens to us when we reach old age?

Cecelia Gross had a way of talking as plain as her looks, but she also had a point. What gave Louisa the right to force her way into people's lives and demand answers? Was it a disinterested quest for the truth, an earnest attempt to dig beneath the surface, to trace the roots of the story?

Her newspaper column Tittle-Tattle involved no digging. It was simply a report of comings and goings, of what people did and what they said. Often enough, what they said revealed more than they intended. It was full of irrelevant details and unexamined assumptions. But keep them talking, and eventually they tell the truth, or what they honestly believe.

Hapsburgers for the most part repeated stock opinions, old stories that acquired the stamp of authority through repetition, and facts they never bothered to verify. These so-called facts were often implausible, sensational, and cruel. Someone was a saint for repressing normal behavior, while someone else got what they deserved. Gossip was a key to emotions and attitudes. As a source of information, it had to be strained, like a simmering soup pot of bones and trimmings.

Louisa made herself a sandwich and ate it at the kitchen table. Jasper lay on the floor at her feet. She reviewed the notes she had scribbled during the past two days. Her own handwriting was difficult to read. It veered in all directions and got tangled in knots like a wayward thread of yarn. To listen to someone talk and record the words simultaneously was a challenge. Accuracy was vital. If she misquoted someone, he or she was sure to resent it. Like Cecelia Gross, they would correct her in public. In Hapsburg, a high percentage of verbal exchanges consisted of corrections. What exactly was said, to whom, and when, and so on.

As for a coherent line of inquiry, Louisa saw none. She was searching for evidence, not making judgments. Gary Nash is missing. Patrick Willis is secretly present. Either one might have caused Ralph's death, or neither. Ralph had a rough edge, a tart personality. By no means was he sweetness and light. His life extended beyond Hapsburg. An unknown visitor might have come and gone on Sunday night. What disreputable characters lurked in his past? A musical acquaintance involved in drugs? A dropped friend who was mentally disturbed and bent on revenge? What minor offense had festered in the mind of some poor soul until it drove him to murder?

As Captain Ryder said, an armed robbery might have gone wrong. Violent crime was rare, more often seen in movies and television than in real life. But if speculation was out of bounds, why did Ryder mention it? He was embarrassed, that was clear. Because a crime happened on his watch, or because he had something to hide?

"At least you are innocent," Louisa said to Jasper. "And I can't misquote you."

Jasper wriggled and snuffled in protest. "I have plenty to say," he implied. "Look into my big brown eyes."

"There is more to this journalism than I expected," Louisa said. "Maybe there are rules about what a reporter can and should do. Ways to ask questions and ways to connect the answers. I will have to consult my editor."

"Indubitably," Jasper said. This was how Harold had interpreted the dog's grunts and groans. They could carry on a conversation at length.

"Am I barking up the wrong tree?"

To this, Jasper made no reply.

Author's Note

Jasper is made of excerpts from a mystery novel, in which Louisa solves the mystery. The dog stands for her missing husband, but he's still a dog with his own needs. Louisa elsewhere says she is a lonely old woman who talks to her dog. Jasper fills a need in her.

CAMPING WITH FRIENDS

Joseph E. Fleckenstein

Melvin and I both worked for a firm that developed computer pro-grams. That was before the pandemic and the mass layoffs that ensued. Mel-vin was the janitor in the building; I was a programmer. Back then, neither of us found either the time or the interest in speaking to the other. We each had our own set of peers as well as tasks to be addressed. There was, how-ever, one day Melvin and I spoke albeit briefly. I happened to be in the men's room when he was tending plumbing in one of the stalls. He happened to see me nearby and turned to say, "Damn guys. They piss on the seats; too lazy to lift a seat. Where do they find these characters?" All I said was, "Who knows. Characters are everywhere." That was the extent of our conversation until years later when the evolution of events cast us together in a common need to survive.

Our employer gave Melvin and me notice the same day. The Human Resources people herded some fifty of us into a large cavernous room. They were decent about the occasion. I'll give them credit for putting on a good front. The chief Human Resources honcho made a little speech preliminary to the big punch. He said management was "sorry" and truly projected gen-uine regret. Strange, I thought, how he did that. Reflecting on the firing, I often wondered if HR people practice saying how sorry they are for the things they do. At home, do they individually stand before a mirror to test their delivery? Do they meet periodically to practice and test one another? Oh, Linda, try looking sad the whole time you are making your good-by speech. That smile near the end is inconsistent with what we want to project. We need to make employees think we really mean it when we say we are sorry for giving them the boot. Keep smiles for when we are attracting peo-ple to the company not when we want to get rid of them. Let's try that again.

While I was eligible for unemployment checks, I went regularly to the unemployment office. In their facility the state offered listings of job open-ings and other literature free for the taking. Sometimes the unemployment people wanted to talk. Mostly, I determined, they wanted to be sure I was looking for another job. I suppose management had given them their man-dates: Make sure these people are trying to find work. We don't want to send out unemployment checks any more than necessary. Several times I saw Melvin there. We recognized one another and exchanged "hellos" on occasion. I would call Melvin an uncomplicated type. I learned later he had dropped out of high school. Because he had a lisp, the other kids made fun of him. He merely wanted to get away from the people who were constantly making fun of him. He told me he regretted having the lisp, but he could do nothing about it. Despite his limited education, Melvin was nobody's fool. He followed the national and international news with keen interest and was well abreast of the ongoing issues in Washington. Several weeks before the checks were due to run out, we discussed our dilemma in detail and with some urgency.

Melvin and I both gradually came to the same, disappointing conclusion: We would both be unable to afford the rent for our respective apartments once the unemployment checks stopped showing up in our mailboxes. That was when I told Melvin of my intention to move into a tent far east of town. I told him I owned this eight foot wall tent that my ex and I had used on camping trips, and I was going to go camping full time. I said that I had enough money saved to pay for a camping site and food well into the future. I said I thought I had no choice. I was not going to live in the streets with dangerous and unkempt homeless people. I added that I wanted a place with clean bathrooms and showers. My camping plans caught Melvin's attention. He asked a few questions, and I could see he was becoming seriously interested in my game plan.

The next time I saw Melvin at the unemployment office he seemed unusually pleased to see me. He smiled when he saw me which was in contrast with his normal dour demeanor. After a few pleasantries, he told me he liked my camping plans and, in fact, had priced a tent. Events developed rapidly from that time on. Two weeks later, Melvin and I packed up what few possessions we could keep in a tent. I left my furniture and other belongings for the landlord. I figured that to some extent he could use the items as part payment toward the rents I hadn't paid the last few months. I didn't know what Melvin did with his belongings. Sometimes it's best to avoid asking too many personal questions. I'll say this: Everything he brought fit easily into the trunk of my car. Melvin didn't own a car, so I volunteered to drive him and his gear to the campground. The drive east and up into the mountains took ninety minutes. We arrived on a beautiful, sunny day in July. In the distance I could see snow-capped mountains. Those mountains were beautiful to behold, but the snow served to remind us cold weather would arrive one day. I negotiated a good rate at the campground. I explained to the owner that we needed two sites and, in addition, we were planning on staying long-term.

I took a site near the bathrooms, the showers and the front office. If I had to go in the middle of the night, I didn't want to be stumbling along a muddy path and tripping over tree roots. Melvin said he liked the calmness of the woods and selected a spot at the rear of the property. It was just as well that our tents were separated by a good distance. If we were side-by-side, we might soon grow tired of one another's company.

Our first evening at the campground, Melvin came over to my new quarters. I had brought two kitchen chairs with me from my apartment: One for the occasional guest and one for me. Although the confines of the tent allowed little room for possessions, I considered two substantial chairs a necessity. I opened a bottle of pinot noir from my collection, and we toasted our new way of life. The wine seemed to loosen Melvin's tongue. He became uncharacteristically talkative. He told me he was the youngest of three children. His mother raised her brood after his father left the house one night and didn't come back. He spoke lovingly of his mother and I noticed a tear appear in the corner of his eye. Melvin was a good conversationalist. He read all kinds of periodicals and books and could speak knowingly on a range of subjects. Unlike most of my former co-workers, he didn't try to impress with tales of accomplishment or his sundry collection of wonderful possessions. He showed sincere interest in other people's opinions and aspirations. Being a former janitor, he also displayed a mechanical inclination. He noticed what he called problems with the drainage around the outside of my tent and made certain corrections. He explained that the way I had the drainage arranged I would have most certainly experienced wet feet at the first rain.

Melvin and I settled into the routine of life in a campground. I would have a granola bar and water for breakfast. I skipped lunch because it was too much trouble finding and preparing something to eat. Most mornings I would go for a walk in the hills behind the campground. I had always enjoyed hiking and taking in nature's scenery. Often I saw wildlife on my treks. All kinds of songbirds, deer. One morning I saw a weasel scurry after a wood rat. Skunks, too. Since our arrival at the campground, the weather had been nothing but wonderful. The dry and crisp air of the mountains lifted the spirit. Of course, we both knew staying warm during the coming cold weather would be a challenge. We both agreed we would worry about that particular challenge at a later day. Perhaps we both secretly thought and hoped that in time we might find an alternative to living in a tent in cold weather.

In our new way of life, Melvin and I didn't find many pleasures. Nevertheless, we decided eating well would be one of them. Much to my surprise,

Melvin and I became good friends. More than anything, our friendship was based on a common need to survive without a regular source of income. I already owned a two-burner Coleman camp stove. Melvin bought a single burner. He said that if he needed a second burner, then he would buy another one-burner. In the evenings both Melvin and I prepared a cooked meal. I usually made a trip to the valley every two or three days to buy groceries. We had no way to keep food other than canned goods, but neither of us used canned food that much. On each trip to the valley I bought only what we needed for the next two or three days. Once a week, we would get together for a meal with a special entrée. One week, Melvin would make a meal for two at his tent, the next week would be my turn. The guest cook would provide a bottle of wine; that was the rule. On occasion, we would invite another resident of the campground for supper. Despite our limited means, we both consistently made meals that were both appetizing and nutritious.

After several of our get-togethers, I started to wonder about Melvin's sexual orientation. Unlike heterosexual men I had ever known, he never mentioned women. Some men, I learned, are more explicit with friends than others, quick to talk about fast women, one night stands or special conquests of the past. Other men will mention wives or former girlfriends in a more courtly manner. Nevertheless, most men are inclined to eventually discuss women and sex. To compare notes so to speak. It's in the male DNA. Not so with Melvin. Although I tried to gingerly broach the subject, he didn't seem inclined to respond. He never suggested that he thought about women to any degree. Could it be that he was gay? Or merely asexual? The love he declared for this mother seemed characteristic of a homo. Whatever his bent, I concluded I would avoid further mention of women to him. In our present prediction we both needed a trustworthy and reliable companion. I thought that my mentioning his avoidance of the subject might engender animosity or resentment.

In time, Melvin and I both met other people at the campground. A few were typical campers - people we envied, people with employment and a house elsewhere. Those types stayed at the campground a mere few days or a week before departing. Melvin and I would say a friendly "hello" but otherwise didn't bother to engage transients in conversation. A few of the newcomers to the campground had given up their comfortable places of abode due to necessity and, much as Melvin and I, came to the conclusion that life in a campground was an acceptable alternative to other dreadful options. Some continued to stew in the gloom of their bad luck and stayed to themselves. We avoided those types.

One day Melvin told me a middle aged woman moved into the campground near his stand. To make her acquaintance, I walked to her tent and introduced myself. She told me she was also from the West Coast. She had been a graphics designer before she was terminated. She was attractive with long black hair and dark brown eyes. Somewhat business-like and prissy. Said her name was Regina. We chatted a few minutes and, to my surprise, she asked if there was a shooting range nearby. I suspected her purpose was to advertise that she could ably protect herself and with deadly force if need be. I told Regina I didn't know of a shooting range, but I told her to simply go in the woods behind the campground and do her practice there. Find a big tree and let it have it. I told her Melvin and I were having beef bourguignon at my place that Friday and she was welcome. I told her we would consider the event her welcoming party. That brought a smile, and she seemed delighted at the invitation. She said she would be over and asked if she should bring anything. I told her "No, just yourself."

For Regina's welcoming party, I borrowed a third chair so that the three of us could sit when we ate and, perhaps, drank. Regina was early for dinner and brought along a fresh gallon of Gallo mountain burgundy. We started on the wine well before the beef was ready. By dinnertime we had big appetites. I received numerous compliments on my cooking. After dinner, we had more wine. What the hell, none of us had any place to go to other than our lonely tents. Conversation came easily as the wine flowed. We compared notes on the campground and, the concern in the back of our minds, how to cope with the coming cold weather. I volunteered that having ample wine handy would help. Regina became nostalgic talking about a boyfriend she had only the prior year. A boyfriend who disappeared into the fog. She could show a sharp edge at times. When talking about her last employer, she peppered her speech with words as "bastards," "mothers," and "child molesters." I told Regina I had no such feeling toward my past employer. Business was business and "those people" did what they had to do in their everlasting quest to make a buck. I said I held out hope my last employer would call me back some day.

The day after the party, I stayed mostly on my cot. A wine hangover is the worst kind. I had a lingering headache and nausea throughout the day. By midnight I had a slight appetite, but I didn't eat anyway. The following day I was up and about although still walking gingerly. I drove down to McDonald's in the valley and ordered a hamburger for breakfast – my first hamburger in five years. Afterward, I went for a drive to tour the roads in the area. That afternoon, I walked over to Melvin's tent. The flap on the tent was open because it was a hot day. Melvin was reclined on his cot, and initially I turned to leave as I didn't wish to wake him. Apparently he was not sleeping and he called to me, "Don't go. I was going to pay you a visit anyway." He added the obvious: "I think we had too much wine the other night. Next time I'm going to have to keep score better. It was Regina's fault. I'm blaming our hangovers on her." Melvin stood and walked to the corner of his tent where he had a case of wine. He withdrew a bottle of a California Chardonnay and worked the cork loose. He handed me a paper cup with the wine and told me, "This will make you feel better."

The onset of cooler weather prompted me to consider some kind of heat for my tent. I discussed my problem with the owner of the campground who suggested a coal-burning camp stove. He explained wood stoves are cheaper than wood stoves and wood can be obtained free, but a coal fire lasts longer. With wood, a person must tend to the fire at least once or twice during a cold night. On the other hand, a coal fire will last throughout the night. I told both Regina and Melvin I was going to order a coal-burning stove. Both asked me to also order one for them; I did although I didn't think either would actually pay me. Time proved me correct. Melvin, handyman that he was, modified all three tent roofs to accommodate stove pipes.

Regina kept busy chilly days drawing in her tent, practicing at a genuine talent. Melvin was into crossword puzzles, jigsaw puzzles and books. Mostly, I read. Melvin also retrofitted all three tents with windows so that we had adequate light inside our tents for whatever we wanted to see or do. Regina said she wanted to be part of our weekly cook fest, so we made our club a club of three. Time proved her the best of the three cooks. Once she had two glasses of wine, she loosened up and in fact became entertaining. Her repertoire of jokes was both surprising and entertaining.

The campground had a heated rec room with a TV and hi-fi. When the cold weather and snow arrived, the three of us spent most winter days within the confines of that room. On occasion, I noticed each of my companions staring out at the snow, thinking or daydreaming. I often wondered if they were each thinking of certain pleasant days of the past, days when they each had employment, friends and a place they called home. Or was it their current dilemma that caused their minds to wander? I, too, caught myself looking out those windows and concentrating on the snow for long periods. At night the rec room was closed to all, and then we were obliged to return to our tents.

Author's Note:

Why write anything, really? I have long found encouragement to write stories that will entertain and a way inspire. I try to piece together tales with irony, humor and puzzles related to what we all encounter in our mutual efforts to find happiness and contentment in our lives. Briefly stated, my intent was to write a story with an entertaining plot.

THE BRIDGE

John Riebow

The hard ground felt reassuring under Russell Mitchell's feet as he jogged over the Spring Garden Street Bridge. It was great to be out of the house, if only for a while. The streets of Philadelphia were mostly empty this time of the night, except for the rare car or odd bundle of homeless atop a steaming vent. It was a beautiful October night and Mitchell wanted to get out over the river, which was often draped in a fine mist when there was a sudden temperature change, as there had been that afternoon.

He left his Fairmount twin, passing under the leafless London Plane trees that surrounded the Art Museum and lined the parkway, heading out onto the bridge. The night was clearer than expected and the heavyset figure leaning on the railing stood out. The man, in dark pants and bulky sweatshirt, was somewhat of an imposing figure on the deserted street. Mitchell, instinctively wary, noticed the hooded figure was actually slumped over the railing and seemed to be peering into the river, as if mesmerized. He crossed the bridge and headed back toward the parkway, but as he took a circuit around the Eakins Oval, something drew him back over the bridge, where the figure remained. He chided himself for his morbid curiosity. At second look, the sight was more disturbing than threatening, and Mitchell began to ask questions. Was the person hurt, or merely drunk? Should he ask if he could help, or give the man a little nudge? He could just move on, go back home and forget all, but his Eagle Scout intuition wouldn't let him. With cell phone at the ready to dial 911, he moved closer.

"Nice night." Mitchell huffed, feigning a leg stretch on the railing about five feet from the hunched individual. "I love it when it's this quiet."

The figure turned slightly, revealing a glimpse of profile, and it was the first time he realized the man was Black. Not that it mattered to him, or was surprising, he just wasn't thinking. It was a slight look, not dismissive or threatening. The man, who from the brief glance appeared to be about a decade older than Mitchell's thirty years, resumed his contemplation of the flowing Schuylkill River.

"It's a little chilly for this time of the year. I don't know about you, but I like a bit of a nip in the air. It's refreshing. Hurts the lungs and makes you snot up a bit, but it's stimulating."

Mitchell took a deep breath but his exaggerated exhale did not draw attention.

"Man, it's really clear tonight. Even with all the lights, you can still see a lot of stars. You can just make out the Big Dipper over there," he pointed. The bundled individual looked up briefly. "See it?"

Encouraged by the figure's mild interest, Mitchell continued.

"I love the view from here—that's why I go this way—just to see those buildings, those lights, the way the river snakes between the skyline. I run this way on purpose. I go up and down the parkway, but just have to get up on this bridge. The view is too awesome."

The figure remained motionless and silent.

"It's a lovely city, isn't it? It looks so peaceful at night, almost like a painting. Hard to believe it can be so ugly during the day—with all those people getting killed. Didn't we set some sort of murder rate record last year? It's sad, really sad."

Mitchell believed there was a faint murmur of agreement. He leaned against the railing, contemplated the skyline.

"You know, you don't see the corruption, the abuse and the city hall kickbacks from here. In fact, you can just about see City Hall since they put up all these other buildings. Do you remember when no building was allowed to be taller than William Penn's hat?"

The figured faced him as if to say, 'why the hell are you telling me all this?' but said nothing.

"I remember my uncle being so outraged at the prospect. He grew up here, worked as a driver for Greyhound, and thought the world was going to spin off its axis if a building was built higher than the damned hat. I don't know what was so damned special about that damned hat, but I like the new skyline. It has a... presence, a power. Can you imagine what it would be like if there were a bunch of squatty buildings lower than William Penn's damned hat? It wouldn't be the same, would it? Then again, the Eagles haven't won a Super Bowl, so maybe there is something to that curse."

Mitchell knew his rambling exhibited the worst kind of sign to a would-be attacker: fear, but there was something about the hunched figure that was more dejected than threatening.

"The city definitely has a majesty to it, don't you think?" A gesture that may have been a shrug spurred him on. "The new buildings are modern. They look world-class and speak to me of progress. They make a distinctive mark that says 'man was here.' I mean, just look at that Cira Center over

there! Magnificent! And I know a little about buildings because I'm an architect. I look like an architect, don't I? I bet you thought I was an accountant—
that's just the glasses. I could never be an accountant—I'm shit at math."

Mitchell slapped the railing and gave a self-deprecating laugh, his mild
fear melting.

"I've always loved putting things together, but I'm terrible with my
hands—I'm all thumbs," he said, waving hands with fingers curled in. "I can't
even hang a bookshelf, or worse yet, put together IKEA furniture, without
doing myself some damage. I knew I couldn't be a carpenter or a mason, or
a plumber, but did have a knack for figuring out how things went together,
and could draw a bit, so I went to school and became an architect. I just
passed my license exam last year, so it's official."

If Mitchell had been expecting some manner of congratulations, it
never came. The man was leaning sideways on the railing, face knitted in
contemplation as to why this skinny little white boy would be telling his life
story to a Black man in the middle of the night.

"That's one of the reasons I stayed after graduating from Penn—because
I fell in love with the city: the history, the art, and the architecture. I also fell
in love with Ellie, my wife, but that's another matter. It was the city that first
stole my heart. Man, there are some amazing buildings around here, everywhere you look. Having grown up outside of Wilkes-Barre, I never knew
anything so exciting and beautifully dangerous. It's a great city. The politi-
cians and sports teams suck, but it's a great city. The people are awesome. Are
you from around here, or are you a transplant like me?"

Mitchell was surprised to get a reply. "Born and raised near 43rd and
Market." The man said in a deep voice, pulling back his hood to reveal a
graying head of short-cropped hair.

"Ah, a local then," the architect said, pleased to have finally been
engaged. "So, you've seen how things have changed over the years?"

"I have," the figure acknowledged.

"I think change is good. I know a lot of people who don't like change,
but life is about change, isn't it? We're always changing, from the moment
we are born. We never stay the same. I used to have a full head of hair and
good eyesight."

"I was forty pounds lighter," the man joked, patting his stomach
good-naturedly.

"You see—change! So tell me, were you going to jump into the river?" Mitchell asked suddenly.

The figure pronounced, without hesitation, looking down into the water, "I was considering it."

"You could do yourself some serious damage doing that," Mitchell said with a disapproving shake of head. "I bet the water's friggin cold this time of year. You could get hypothermia. It's pretty shallow too, and there are a lot of rocks; you'd most likely bash your head. There's a wicked undertow in this part as well. You'd be sucked down to the Delaware and out into the shipping lane. They'd probably never find you. It's also the Schuylkill—it's disgusting."

"Yeah," the figure agreed with a sad nod and spat into the darkness below.

"Were you trying to kill yourself?"

The reply came without hesitation. "The thought had crossed my mind."

"Mind my asking why you'd want to do such a thing?"

"Guess not," the man shrugged but remained silent.

"So? Why?"

"Things are just really fucked up at the moment," the confession came in a sigh.

"Oh, is that all?" Mitchell said with a relieved smile. "Things are really fucked up for everyone. They are for me. That's why I'm out here at three in the morning. Don't you think I'd be tucked up in my warm bed with the wife if things weren't really shitty?"

"Couldn't sleep?"

"No. Every time I close my eyes I see the blackness, like a movie screen, and then the images start."

"Really? No bullshit?"

"Word! There are no previews—it goes straight to the main feature, which is me running down this hill. I'm running through this sort of jungle and have to fight my way through low branches and vines, and all these hostile natives with spears are chasing me. They are screaming, shooting poison darts and getting closer. It's kinda like the opening of the first Indiana Jones movie."

"What happens?"

"I don't know," Mitchell confessed with a bemused shrug. "I lay there for hours, playing this chase scene out, over and over. I'm just running. It never ends. And when I finally do get to sleep, the alarm usually goes off. I couldn't take it anymore tonight and thought a little reality run could tire me out."

"Do the natives ever chase you when you're running out here in the middle of the night?" the man asked with a wicked grin.

"Are you being racist?"

"I'm Black—if Chris Rock can poke fun at the brothers, so can I. Why do you keep having this dream? A lot on your mind?"

"Yeah."

"Love or money?"

"Both." Mitchell admitted. "Things have been a little rough the last year or so. My daughter Tracy has a malformed hip. She's been in and out of casts, back and forth to the doctors, and now we're contemplating a hip replacement. The poor kid's been through a lot, and she's only three. I feel for her, but it's also tough on Ellie and me. I never thought we'd fight like we do. I never expected her to call me an asshole."

"That's nothing, I'm a fucking prick, so SHE says."

"Sometimes we get into these huge screaming matches, over the stupidest things, for no other reason than we're tired. Yesterday I yelled at her for buying the wrong shaving cream, and tonight she told me I was an asshole because I explained Tracy's condition wrong when I was telling the neighbor what was going on."

"The running dream makes sense, man."

"Really?"

"For real."

"I dig you, man. Do you think I could join you?" Mitchell asked, moving closer to the older figure.

"What?"

"Can I jump with you? We wouldn't have to hold hands or anything— that would be a little gay—but maybe we could count off together and jump at the same time, just to give one another a little moral support."

"You're one crazy cracker!" the man said with a dismissive wave of hand.

"I'm serious. Apart from the water being completely disgusting, it's not a bad way to go, I guess. Better than dying in a house fire or car crash. The only problem with jumping in the river is that the old body doesn't look too pretty after it's been floating in water for a few days, especially something as primordial as the Schuylkill."

"You said you just became what, an architect? Why would you want to jump?"

"I never imagined it was going to be like this," Mitchell said, reflecting. "I thought getting through school was going to be the hard part of life. I got married and expected things to run their course: I'd get a little house, have a kid or two, maybe a dog, but it's never that simple, is it? Not like it seems when you're a kid imagining what your adult life is going to be like. We don't think about a surly boss, backstabbing coworkers, unbearable in-laws, the mortgage weighing you down, and putting up with fifty weeks of bullshit just to get two weeks off to wiggle your toes in the sand. No, you don't think about any of that when you're a kid. Good thing too, or we'd never grow up and leave our parents' houses."

The night grew silent as both men reflected. After a long moment, the older man began, "My son is talking about joining up, going into the Army. He doesn't have the grades for college. He barely got through high school. He's tired of working odd jobs that aren't going to get him anywhere. He says there's nothing for him here, and knows he's going to get wrapped up with the wrong crowd if he just hangs out. Philly's like quicksand that way: you gotta keep moving or get sucked under. I'm terrified if he does join up, he's just going to be more meat for the grinder in Iraq. You'd expect to get shot over there, but out here it's a war too, every day, an undeclared war, with everyone shooting at everything. It's not easy being young and Black."

"I wouldn't want to be a young person today—of any color." Mitchell admitted, "and for the record, I ain't that old."

There was a heavy sigh and sudden movement. Despite his size, the older figure slid deftly over the railing, as a stunned Mitchell moved to grab his legs.

"I'm not going to let you jump," the young man declared. "You can do it after I leave, but not while I'm here."

"Don't you have somewhere else to be?" The question was matter-of-fact.

"Not at the moment."

"I thought if I was gone Darren would have to stay," the man sobbed as he quivered on the railing. "He wouldn't join, wouldn't go away. He'd stay and look after his mother and sister. Maybe he could get my job at the plant. They'd get by on my little insurance policy. It sucks, but I'm worth more dead than alive."

"Don't say that. It's not true."

"As much as I'm worried about Darren, I don't even want to tell you about my daughter, Kia. She's going to be the next American Idol, whether we like it or not!" The old man managed a choked laugh through tears.

Mitchell climbed up on the railing and stood side by side with the man. "Tell me about her. Tell me about Kia," he urged.

"Say, what the hell are you doing, man?" the figure asked, suddenly panicked as the two swayed precariously above the black waters below.

"I just want to see it, what it's like up here, to see if I could really do it."

"Could you?" the older man asked, looking at his younger counterpart through earnest tears.

"No," Mitchell admitted with a vehement shake of head, moisture welling in his eyes. "It would hurt my wife and daughter too much. They'd assume I'd done it because of them."

"I never thought of that. My family would probably blame each other if I jumped. It would tear them apart, not bring them closer together," the man said, extending a hand to Mitchell. "I'm Malcolm, by the way."

"Russ. Pleased to meet you."

"Likewise, Russ."

"Do you think we can get down now? I have a touch of vertigo and suddenly feel like hell."

Laughing, the two jumped to the sidewalk, slapping one another on the back.

"Hey, someone could get hurt up there," Malcolm announced, panting nervously. "The hell with this shit. I'm going home, get some sleep."

"Cool. Me too. One more lap around the Oval and I'm gone. I wish it would have been under better circumstances, but I'm glad we ran into one another. If you ever want to grab a beer sometime—"

"You know, I really don't have nothing against you white boys, except you talk way too much."

"Right," Mitchell said, taking the hint.

The hard ground felt reassuring under Russell Mitchell's feet as he jogged over the Spring Garden Street Bridge, down the parkway, and headed toward home. He was going to wake up his wife, listen to her complain about losing sleep, and tell her that he loved her.

Author's Note

I wrote the story about two people using a bridge for different reasons: one to get somewhere, the other to get away. It's also a reflection on people from two completely different backgrounds and experiences having similar thoughts and problems.

MAKE BELIEVE

Amy Suzanne Parker

The dust flies from the furniture, stirred up by a cloth in my hand as Michael Jackson's *Bad* blasts in my parents' bedroom. I breathe in too much lemon Pledge and cough. The cassette player is on high volume, and Mom, my brother, and I sing and clean to the beat of "The Way You Make Me Feel." I try to moonwalk on the bathroom tile, my socks helping my feet slide a little.

I am disappointed. The tile isn't slippery enough. I'm not nimble enough.

I am seven years old when he is accused of child molestation by Jordan Chandler. I don't understand it; I just know bad people do it. Strangers. Never go off with someone you don't know. Fairy tales, school assemblies, and my parents drill this into me.

I don't remember any stranger trying to take me away. My childhood is happy, filled with an out-of-tune ukulele I drive my parents insane with, a pink bedroom complete with a canopy bed, and a stuffed animal leopard named Goldie. She is my companion, and when I am sad, she soaks up my tears well.

Goldie is special. My grandpa donated to the World Wildlife Organization, sponsoring a leopard, just so I could have her. My brother, Tim, has one of those Disney stuffed animals of a Dalmatian. His name is Lucky. Goldie and Lucky are our favorite toys, and we bring them on sleepovers at our grandparents' house.

Grandpa makes peanut butter fudge and popcorn balls. My grandparents sit in their recliners, Tim sits on the floor, and I sit on the couch. Fresh from Blockbuster, we watch *The Nightmare Before Christmas*. The snot-filled burlap blob character freaks me out, but not nearly as much as E.T.

I don't remember when I first saw *E.T., The Extraterrestrial*, but I am so terrified, my dad keeps the VHS hidden in the bottom drawer of a nightstand in my parents' bedroom. When I am feeling bold, I pull out the tape and gaze at the creepy cover—the moon with a shadow of a boy and an alien on a bicycle.

E.T.'s long neck (remember when it stretches upon seeing Drew Barrymore?) and long fingers are what mostly bother me. His huge eyes and the little stump of him don't help. He is wrinkly and brown and secretly evil.

June 2015: I am in La Grande attending Eastern Oregon University for my Master of Fine Arts in creative writing. My goal in life is to outlive Sylvia Plath, and at 29, I'm almost there.

During one cloudy afternoon, Trevor Dodge comes to visit. He asks us if we remember the Atari *E.T.* video game. Gamers contend that it's the worst video game ever, and there's a mound in New Mexico where the copies that didn't sell are buried.

He reads an essay about playing the video game before, after, and while his cousin raped him. He calls it the "Worst *Fucking* Game Ever."

In August that same year, I have a nightmare containing explicit details of sexual abuse I wake up suicidal. I hold an orange bottle of Klonopin in front of the mirror and tilt it but stop before any pills come out. Instead, I plug "Tampa General Hospital" into Google Maps on my phone. I drive in the dark, the sunshine before sunrise lighting up the sky, tears blurring my vision.

In the examination room, I think about the man who bought me a Barbie car I could drive around the block in but only forwards. He would walk beside me, and when the sidewalk ran out, he'd lift up the car and turn it around so I could drive back.

This was the man who walked up to the grocery store and got me raspberries and kiwis, my favorite fuzzy fruits, when I'd been extra good.

This was the man who spent weeks on end trying to find me a teddy bear that looked exactly like Snuggles from the fabric softener commercials.

This was a man who endured the Great Depression in West Virginia, one of the hardest hit states, and who was drafted into the Army during World War II, part of Brokaw's Greatest Generation.

This was a man who likely suffered from severe depression and obsessive-compulsive disorder who only knew alcohol as a means to medicate.

This was a man who taught hundreds of schoolchildren, including one of my psychiatrists.

He was the one who lifted me up and carried me on his shoulders when I got too tired of walking and complained that I couldn't go on because I had "a bone in my leg."

He was the one who took my brother and me to Taylor Park where he'd watch us get dizzy on the merry-go-rounds, burn our thighs on summer slides, and fantasize about swinging to the moon, while behind us, pushing us on the swing set.

He was my grandpa.

I shiver, not knowing if it's from the chilly hospital room or last night's nightmare. I tell the nurses and the social worker he was the one who sexually abused me.

The social worker asks me to describe the trauma. I do, teary-eyed and heaving. With each breath, I feel as if I'm exhaling myself out of my body until I am a balloon drifting away.

"It's about forgiveness," she says.

I nod and look down at the linoleum.

"It's not about forgiving *him*, though—it's about forgiving yourself. Do you blame yourself because you think you let it happen?"

Another nod.

"You were a child. It wasn't your fault."

Her face and words float through my head after she leaves.

During Trevor's reading, I realize something—yes, epiphanies are corny, but they happen. My grandpa had wrinkly, brown skin, a long neck, and gnarled, arthritic fingers.

In the 2019 documentary, *Leaving Neverland*, Wade Robson and James Safechuck recount the sexual abuse they (allegedly) endured at the hands of Michael Jackson. At 50:25 the camera shows a poster with various figures, including Jackson, Einstein, Lincoln, and E.T. with sunglasses on in a bedroom at Neverland Ranch while James Safechuck describes the different places in Jackson's house where they had sex.

In his *New York Times* review of the documentary, Wesley Morris writes:

> *[Jackson] tells the Safechucks how lonely he is. And so, in an alarming throwaway detail, the family starts disguising Jackson in order to sneak him out of Hayvenhurst, his pre-Neverland estate, and into their normal, suburban house. It's like he actually was E.T.*

When Michael Jackson appears with E.T. on television, it frightens me. He narrated the audiobook for the film, and the NYT article links to an *Ebony* article in which Jackson explains his attachment to the alien.

> *He's in a strange place and wants to be accepted—which is a situation that I have found myself in many times when travelling from city to city all over the world. He's most comfortable with children, and I have a great love for kids. He gives love and wants love in return, which is me. And he has that super power which lets him*

lift off and fly whenever he wants to get away from things on Earth,
and I can identify with that. He and I are alike in many ways.

When I told my mom why I was hospitalized, she says she put the idea in my head when she told me that she found Grandpa lying on top of me one day. I don't recall her ever saying anything to me about this—this is after the flashbacks and nightmares. I take this as evidence.

Days after, when I talk to her again, she admits it might've happened. It might've happened to her, too.

I don't know what to believe. I don't know whom to believe—myself or my mother. My own memory is highly fallible, I admit, after years of antidepressants, antipsychotics, and electroconvulsive therapy. The SSRIs and atypical antipsychotics mess with my recall, and depression itself fucks up my memory. The main side effect of ECT is short-term memory loss, but after having it throughout my 20s, this effect has staying power. However, the memory loss only affects the immediate time period around the procedure, not memories before or after.

I don't remember having flashbacks, nightmares, or memories of any abuse until I am 28, after my last round of ECT for my fifth major depressive episode.

And so, I doubt myself.

On the website for the British magazine *Spiked!*, Joanna Williams writes in an article titled, "The Make-Believe World of Child Abuse Campaigners": "Children of [5 years old] want answers to everything, but they also want to make-believe." After discussing "vastly inflated data" of "sordid fantasy" and mocking schools who teach students about age-appropriate relationships, she continues, "Today it seems that five-year-olds are not allowed the luxury of make-believe and must instead have 'lessons in life.'"

I was an imaginative girl, acting out plots from *Days of Our Lives* with my Barbies on the brown carpet next to the small table where Tim and I used to sit in the TV room at my grandparents' house. One day I got frustrated and cut off my Cinderella Barbie's hair. I dressed her in mismatched, skimpy clothing and pretended she was a whore.

In *The Chronology of Water*, Lidia Yuknavitch writes, "The more a person recalls a memory, the more they change it. Each time they put it into language, it shifts. The more you describe a memory, the more likely it is that you are making a story that fits your life, resolves the past, creates a fiction you can live with."

The nightgown with cornflowers on it has tiny fuzz balls—I feel them rub against my skin. I must be a toddler. Two? Almost? The sleeves have elastic bands. They snap. My skin stings.

I'm wearing a diaper. Latebloomer. Hard to train, eager to please.

Like a damn dog.

The poodle, Cocoa, snaps at and bites me. We compete for my grandfather's attention.

He gives the dog flavored sticks it can chew up.

He gives me Dum Dums I can lick and chew up.

Little succulent spheres with an elevated equator that I crunch and smash between baby teeth. It's okay if I break one on candy. They're not permanent. It won't leave a scar. My mother still discourages it.

There's a twin bed in the living room, more like the sitting room, the TV room where my grandparents watch *Golden Girls*, *Wheel of Fortune*, and *Jeopardy!* while Mom attends nursing school and leaves me and my brother with them.

Two? Tim would have been barely alive. I must be older. Maybe I'm wearing panties instead of a diaper and have confused the stretchy elastic bands on my underwear with my nightgown. There's a laugh track for sitcoms I hear in the background.

One dark, blinds-closed afternoon, my grandmother and Tim are off somewhere else. Maybe this was before Tim was born? Anyway, he's not there. Maybe my grandma is giving him a bath. Maybe they're walking up to the Publix, Tim in stroller. The point is, they are absent, and I am left alone in my nightgown and diaper or panties in the oddly placed twin bed with my grandpa.

In my head, I see this little girl and him. The girl looks like me.

It's 2019, and over the phone, my mother, newly 67, tells me that she has just been diagnosed with cirrhosis of the liver, and I immediately think of my grandpa.

When I was born, Grandpa was in the hospital for cirrhosis. Someone, I presume my father, brought me to his bedside. Story goes, my newborn fingers touched his, and in that very moment, he decided to quit drinking—a kind of E.T. moment.

Now I imagine him jaundiced, barely alive though younger, 67, in fact, his eyes yellow, his sallow skin in the fluorescent light, him dying of cirrhosis. Did he see me, who I would be? Did he read the same dependence and decide to take advantage even then? The little girl in my head asks, is forever asking.

But now that I'm older, I think he did see our meeting as a sign, a moment of truth. He could reform, remake his image, be an amazing grandfather, had all the hope in the world for a rebirth, a resurrection.

The liver can handle a lot.

Maybe he fucked up, couldn't keep his promise, just like the rest of us. Maybe he didn't know if he would live.

On the phone, my mom's voice brings me back to the present, and she deadpans, "We get all the bad genes from Daddy Dearest's side of our family. We got 'em all."

In many other comments on *Leaving Neverland* on Google Reviews, people bring up that both Robson and Safechuck denied Jackson molested them in a 2005 trial. Why would they lie then? That means they are lying now.

In their 1998 article "From Memories of Abuse to the Abuse of Memories" in the anthology, *Truth in Memory*, Jean-Roch Laurence, Duncan Day, and Louise Gaston argue against Freud's theory of memory repression. They conclude, "[A]mnesia is a rare consequence of childhood abuse in children" (331). Repression is a fiction, they argue.

Memory is malleable, fallible, inconsistent. Our imagination can skew it to fit our purpose, like I made my Cinderella Barbie ugly to make myself feel better about my own body. Having no recollection of certain events in my 20s when friends or family members reminisce feels like there are holes in my life I can't ever fill on my own, but even before that, I created a narrative in which I only inherited my severe depression from the genes on my grandpa's side and nothing else.

It's 2016, and I'm telling my psychiatrist about the abuse—she is the first of my psychiatrists I tell. She asks what Grandpa did for a living.

"He was a teacher and administrator at elementary and middle schools."

"What was his name?"

"Samuel Smith."

A pause.

"Did he teach at Oak Grove?"

"I don't know. He taught in Pinellas County."

"Did he teach science?"

"Maybe. I think so. Physics and chemistry."

"I had a science teacher named Mr. Smith in junior high. He was sallow—his eyes were yellow. You could tell he was an alcoholic."

"He was an alcoholic."

"He acted strangely."

Then I tell her his history, why my mother's family moved to Florida.

"He was a teacher at an elementary school in West Virginia, where the family is from. This was in the '50s, so corporal punishment happened. He supposedly paddled two girls so hard and so much that they could not sit down. He was forced to resign."

My psychiatrist believes me.

The last time my mom and I talk about it—over the phone in late 2016—she says, "I don't remember anything ever happening." It was just that one time he was on top of me.

I am going through therapy for the trauma and take medications daily as I have for the last eighteen and a half years. My previous therapist said, "It doesn't matter if it happened or not. What matters is that you believe it happened, and that has affected you and continues to affect you now."

I believe Safechuck and Robson.

In November 2018, I watch *E.T.* When he's sick and white and the sunflowers are dying, I picture my grandpa in his hospital bed when he was dying in 2013. I remember him wrapped up in sheets and blankets, swaddled just like the alien in Elliott's bike basket, before he died. That's the last image I have of him while he was alive. Shrouded, straining.

In 2013, my mother does not attend the funeral. My dad, brother, and I do. I don't cry, though I feel I should, so I conjure some fake tears. I was his favorite grandchild. To my knowledge, I am the only grandchild he abused. I wonder, though, especially after we found out my cousin Jodi shot herself a few years ago; due to the estrangement between my mom and my aunt, we found out via a Google search for my cousin's name.

My mom and my aunt have not spoken to each other since Grandpa died. My aunt was the favorite daughter, my mother, the "stupid" black sheep. Grandpa was always calling her "stupid." My aunt and her surviving daughter, my cousin, have said nothing but good things about him. My mother has never stepped foot in Pinellas County since. We remain estranged.

Some joke that the reason ECT is so effective is because you forget why you're depressed.

I remember lying down in my twin bed in my apartment in college. I sit for days watching the roaches gather and scatter, old pizza boxes stacked up in the kitchen, and Jimmy John's sandwich wrappers spread out in the bedroom. Throwing away anything feels like I'm throwing part of myself away. I need garbage to be complete. Sometimes I turn on the TV to watch

Wimbledon despite my lack of interest in tennis, there's something about momentum that breaks my heart.

Thoughts of suicide aren't far away. At 20, I overdosed on Klonopin in attempt to kill myself. I woke up devastated. There's a little spirit that whispers in my ear to take pills and sleep into death.

I am on medication. I have great health insurance and good doctors. I have ECT, which works quickly to relieve my hollowness. The country is on the verge of the Great Recession (it's 2008), but it does not affect me until I try to get a job after college. My parents have money, and they let me live at home rent-free.

I recognize my privilege.

Now, I try to imagine the whole country depressed—financially and psychologically. My grandpa, the oldest of four children, would have been 10 years old. Going off research and history classes, I try to imagine life during the Great Depression, as much as I can.

He is a child, around eleven. Hunger devours him. He sees his siblings and parents go without. The hunger twists people's faces into mean-mouthed stares, tiny wrinkles wear in around the mouth. I think of the famous photograph of the *Migrant Mother* and her kids burying their faces in her shoulders. Her lips are mostly straight, except for a tug at the sides, making it a frown. She wonders where the food will come from, how she can support her kids. Did Grandpa ever dream of California, like she did? Did he ever dream of Florida? When things seemed impossible, did he dream of death?

I am a child, around ten. Grandpa keeps a secret stash of Carlo Rossi sangria in the closet. He asks me to put two ice cubes in his drink. The number of ice cubes seems important, and I do it, then lift the heavy glass jug and fill his cup up to the top, like he likes it.

Mom is a child, around twelve. Her parents fight. Her dad is having an affair with the Spanish teacher, and Grandpa asks if she wants a new mommy. She starts salting all food to avoid anything bad from happening.

Michael Jackson is a child in the Jackson 5, and his father is whipping him, telling him he has a fat nose, ready and willing with a belt as punishment for rehearsal mistakes not yet made by Michael and his brothers.

At 21, I sit in an apartment I share with two other girls in Tallahassee and watch *E.T.* in its entirety for the first time. I cry at the end, out of love. That I'm out of the dream of the movie, in the present again.

At 22, my grandpa was drafted into the US Army during World War II. I am not sure, but if memory serves me right, he was a mechanic. Did he readjust screws and machines—I know so little—endlessly until he felt right—just the right number, even? What was his magic number? Mine's eight.

At 22, I had my second major depressive episode and a second round of ECT treatments. I wonder if Grandpa felt the same whirlwind of hopelessness, the black edges tugging at him. I imagine him going back and straightening things and tightening bolts an even number of times. Turning engines on and off repeatedly until things felt right, until he felt that nothing bad would happen. I wonder if this is when he starts drinking.

At 22, Michael Jackson earned the highest royalty rate in music: 37%, at the peak of his success. But he wanted to be a kid, the kid he never got to be. Now, I think of my own childhood, how happy it was, or most of it, from what I can remember.

I wonder if Grandpa was molested as a child. I wonder if he ever attempted suicide. I wonder if OCD came down upon him like a cloud or seeped in slowly, counting touches so many times like it was for me. His sister had ECT, but it was unsuccessful and unmodified, so no muscle relaxants or anesthesia were used during the procedure. She used to wail, "I'm so blue!" I don't remember this, but Mom tells me.

What was my grandpa afraid of? Did he have the same fears as me?

Michael Jackson feared growing up and was determined not to. He surrounded himself with children and make believe. Imagining is the human thing to do, and I'm trying to see my grandpa as a human himself. Did the memories of paddling those two girls haunt him? Did drowning his memories in alcohol help him cope with the images of bruised, bloody girl asses, the poverty he knew as a child, what he did as a father and grandfather?

I don't think Grandpa ever forgave himself.

I think of E.T. and home, how I never want to go back there, to Largo, to the house that belonged to my grandparents. There are photos in my parents' house in Gainesville of him walking beside me, Minnie Mouse ears with a pink bow on my head. The sunlight shines on me, and it's hard to make him out in the shadow. But he is there, holding my hand.

When I visit my parents' house after writing this, I examine the photo. He is not holding my hand; only half of his body is in the frame. He's facing the camera, but he's walking away from me. The picture is real, I am certain, but what else was?

I'll never know which ghostly flashes really occurred. The little girl knows, the adult asks, is forever asking.

THE VALUE OF A $20 BILL

Christine M. Estel

Here you go Buttercup, he'd say as he slipped one into my hand or my coat pocket. Or into my bookbag, or wherever. That's what he did when we drove anywhere together—doing it on the sly, usually in the middle of a story, so I would be unsuspecting. Of course I knew his game.

The money Pop gave me was wasted on hot French fries from the cafeteria, even though I brown-bagged my lunch every day. Some I'd spend on black licorice and Tastykake's lemon pies, two of our favorite convenience-store treats. Sometimes I used it for the occasional mall trip or latest rom-com at AMC. And with time and maturity, I eventually saved a bunch for a rainy day.

Each time I was gifted, I'd say, *Aww, Pop, you don't have to!* to which he'd playfully reply, *Aww, but hunny, yes I do!* Then I'd thank him and we'd both laugh as we moved along. He was a giver, never accepting "no" from me on the subject.

Pop grew up in the Swampoodle neighborhood of North Philadelphia, the only son of five children. His Irish Catholic parents raised him on God and tough love, and while his parents enjoyed pleasantries occasionally, like dining out or attending the opera, the family generally pinched pennies. *But we never missed a meal*, he'd defend in his recollections of childhood, a common theme on our drives.

He'd reminisce about his mother giving him ten cents in the morning for a ginger ale and pack of crackers after school, the little extra she could provide, and how he enjoyed playing basketball with the "publics" (public school kids). His storytelling captivated me, like I had lived it myself.

When we'd drive through Center City, he'd conduct my review: *So remember, the streets are numbered east to west, and don't forget that Broad is technically 14th Street. North to south, almost all names are trees.* He was ensuring I knew my way around, in case of an emergency.

Sometimes we'd have to park on Market Street, generally in a no-park zone, so he could quickly collect his next lot of subpoenas to deliver on behalf of Sweeney & Sheehan. *We'll be okay here*, he'd say, as he slid a "POLICE"-inscribed placard on the dash, a mark of protection against tickets. Once I had my own license, he'd leave the keys in the ignition in case I needed to move. After he'd return, I'd hear more stories about the old buses and trains, the "things that would come to [him] at redlights," his antics during KP duty in the Army. Except he never called it that. It was always "the service," a fitting moniker for a giving man.

I'd learn about Princess Grace of Monaco, as we wound around Kelly Drive and past Boathouse Row, and we'd take drives to Girard College so he could teach me more. If we were up for it, we'd stop at Pat's or Geno's, whatever his mood that day. *I don't discriminate*, he'd joke.

No matter what the drive, or for how long, I always got a $20 bill, a privilege reserved for his first grandchild. At the time, I loved the money, but now I value the lessons and memories he linked to it.

In my rough calculation, I received enough $20 bills throughout my childhood and teens to equal the tallest point of William Penn's hat on City Hall—a couple times over, but likely more. But he gave so much more than that.

I'd give all those $20 bills back in exchange for some more of my grandfather's time and love. That would be priceless.

INSOMNIA; A MIDNIGHT FRESCO

Bobby Caldwell

In the middle of the night, the third shift C.O. stuffs *tomorrow* through the bars of my cell.

A single sheet of paper.

I almost remember hearing it brush against the bars last night. But that was hours ago, when I was still successfully engaged in the act of sleep. My current version of "sleep" consists of a never-ending attempt to find a position novel enough to buy a few more minutes of sweet, sweet, oblivion. Deep down I know it's too late—that there is no such position—and that the morning will soon steal the horizon.

Bastard.

Still, I refuse to open my eyes.

If only my petulance could somehow fortify my ears.

Cell doors as heavy as wrecking balls crank open and slam closed with a rhythm beyond the ability of any single individual involved. The battle cries of early-morning dominoes—games waged over tiny stainless steel tables whose seats have been welded in place to prevent theft, or murder, or anything close to a comfortable sitting position—join the sonic fray. Faceless combatants bark spasms, Pentecostal tongues, to commemorate cut books and trump cards in a contest of spades that will go on in perpetuity. This ante meridiem symphony, the soundtrack to my insomnia, climbs handrails and stairs up the galleries of 9-block and into my cell like time-lapse footage of rust.

I try to will the members of the orchestra dead with my mind.

It never works.

With all the enthusiasm of a drunk lifting his head from a toilet I finally pull myself to a sitting position. A single sheet of typing paper lies facedown on the floor. A callout. A few hours ago the paper was tomorrow. Now it's today. I hardly ever get callouts anymore. It means I have somewhere to be. A series of neurons, tucked somewhere in the folds of my grey matter, fire in just the right order to inspire something between anxiety and annoyance.

I scrape the omen off the floor. It sounds like sandpaper. I need to sweep. I turn it over to have a look at the next twenty-four hours of my life.

CALLOUT / ASSIGNMENT - DESCRIPTION: Creative Writing/ Drama/Choir.

REPORTING STATION: Chapel
DEPARTMENT: Recreation
ARRIVE: 19:00 DEPART: 20:30
Military time.
I hate math.
7pm.
Creative writing.
This time the neurons dance out the program for anticipation.
This morning's meditation will not unfold without pestering thoughts of the unknown tugging at my sleeve.
Back to the breath.
Ignore the distractions.
Stay in the moment.
It almost never works.
The rest of the day passes with the typical monotony of life behind bars—only now I have this looming workshop to get ready for.
I do my best to temper my expectations.
This will be my first creative writing class. The closest I've come is a book called *Elements of Style* by Strunk & White. The librarian at the last joint bought it for me—at least I assume it was her. She was lovely. We'd talk literature. She'd read my stuff and help me with edits. Whenever I'd badger her about some technical writing rule she'd suggest I order this book.
I never did.
Eventually she left. Prison gossip said she'd transferred to a prison closer to home. A few days after she fled, in search of different shades of green, two books came in the mail. One was Victor Frankel's *A Man's Search For Meaning*. She said it reminded her of my writing. The other was *Elements of Style*. There was no name on the package.
Everything else I know about writing I learned from reading and instinct.
Kerouac showed me adventure.
Palahniuk: rebellion.
Vonnegut: irreverent humor.
Bukowski: grit.
Huxley: range.
Salinger: angst.
They showed me style, let me know what was possible if you arranged words in just the right order. Alchemists.

I wondered what wisdom this little callout could impart.

Even with twenty-four hours notice I almost didn't make it. On my way out the door, the C.O. in my unit—the one who's supposed to sign our callouts before we can leave—looks at my itinerary and asks, "Where you going with that?" He uses his pen to point at the JPay tablet strung around my neck. "Can't take that."

My first protest is confusion. My second is, "Why?"

"You don't need that," he says. "It has nothing to do with writing... or singing."

Brilliant.

Before I can mention that the ONLY meaningful capabilities of the little electronic device around my neck are, ironically, the exact two things he claims it has nothing to do with, he slides the callout under the glass partition, unsigned. I've been down long enough to know that any objection based on logic or reason would only succeed in eating up time that I don't really have. So I say nothing.

Three flights up. Three down. Pass signed.

I make it out the door just in time.

Tablet tucked in my back pocket.

I'd never been to the chapel—to any prison chapel actually—but I knew exactly where it was. In the center of the compound sits a small rebellious A-framed building headed in its own direction. It's almost as if all the buildings were headed the same way when the chapel suddenly realized it had lost its keys, turned around to find them, and was suddenly frozen in place.

The chapel's only act of conformity—or insecurity really—is the razor sharp spire rising from the head of its ridge. The mock phallus nearly doubles the height of the independent little building.

I watch an inmate slip through a door in the back of the chapel. I rush to catch up. Inside are two cramped offices that look to have been tacked on long after the church's original construction. A rather congenial C.O. asks for our passes. He delivers his signature line, "Take your hats off." He uses the callouts, curled in his grip, to point to a door.

I'm not wearing a hat.

The inmate ahead of me slides the beanie from his head and into his coat pocket in one fluid motion.

One foot in Kansas, one foot in Oz. I follow him into the chapel.

Years behind bars can lead you to believe that every room, in every building on the planet, is a painfully lit concrete box. I'd completely forgotten that churches—especially old churches—have a welcoming to them that you'd never see in prison.

Structurally, the interior of the chapel is what you'd expect from the outside. No dividing walls. No separate rooms. Just four load-bearing walls and a vaulted ceiling. But, like most things worth knowing, its external simplicity belies a beauty within.

As you step inside the ceiling rises like two massive waves of polished wooden slats. Glistening, as if they'd been dipped in olive oil, the mahogany peaks rush towards each other, climbing, until they finally crash together into a sturdy ridge. Several ceiling fans with nothing much to prove, slowly spin their slick wooden blades over rows of rich mahogany pews below. Everything in here was alive once.

Us included.

Mercifully absent are the screaming fluorescents bulbs whose light dominates, sterilizes every inch of every institution ever built. The chapel lights don't scream, they yawn, radiating a glow you could warm honey with or grow Kentucky Blue grass under. This place is a cozy velvet-lined cigar box. And I am on the verge of converting.

No more than a dozen of us show up for class. Everyone seems to be here for the right reasons—or at least not the wrong ones.

We spend a few minutes marveling in relative silence before our free-world counterparts arrive. Two women from the University of Michigan. There were supposed to be three. One had car trouble. They lead us in silly improv games designed to let us step outside of ourselves, to loosen up and relax. We learn names through movement, string connections with laughter, and convert vulnerability to trust.

The hour and a half class goes by like déja vu. Before I can check the time, or catch my breath, I'm back in my cell halfway through my nightly ritual. I open and close a bag of chips, scan channels, wash my face, squeeze paste on a brush, and select *Recently Added Playlist*. Juice WRLD.

High hat.

Snare.

Kick.

I watch myself brush my teeth in the faded mirror above my sink. The light from the talking heads on my TV gives my skin a bluish glow. My tattoos are subdued. My brush strokes in rhythm with the music.

Spit.

Rinse.

I close the TV and kill my eyes. Laying here, my heart beats a two-step. Flashes of chapel velvet cut with snippets of dialogue, waves, wood, and the rapid unfolding of that little white piece of paper make a firework's show of my neurons.

Sleep seems naive.

Invasive pinholes of light prevent me from reaching back into oblivion. I tie a shirt around my face to lure the darkness necessary for sleep. Failure. The light isn't coming in through the shirt. It's inside of my head, going out. I undo the makeshift sleeping mask and exhale frenetic energy towards the ceiling.

A fresco yet to be painted.

I can almost feel my cells in motion. All this potential energy, this high frequency biology, has to be more than just the lingering effects from the three cups of coffee I slammed before class.

I feel like water on a slick street with downed power lines.

This is about the chapel.

There wasn't one single thing you could pin down about tonight. No monumental happening. But I felt something different over there, something I haven't felt in a long time. Oh god, was it freedom? Am I that fucked up? Has it been so long that I'd forgotten that *freedom* was anything more than a word? CHRIST, I felt a twinge of freedom and didn't even know what to call it!

There was an energy in that little cigar box that was set in motion before any of us even showed up. It might've INVOLVED us, but it didn't COME from us. That type of energy isn't made behind prison walls. It can't be cultivated in the presence of steel bars and razor wire. It is uncorrupted by training or job titles, ignorant to the hatred between convict and institution. This specific brand of energy, formed with idealism, hope, a little higher education, and a couple pairs of X chromosomes was the catalyst. Without the infusion of free energy whose trajectory hasn't yet bent or flagged under the influence of time and its inevitable disappointments we would've been nothing more than a handful of convicts in an old church.

Blasphemous.

Instead—even if it was only for a few consecutive moments—we were allowed to be more than just six digit numbers, more than convicts and case numbers, gang members or college students, fuck ups or saints. Tonight, in that little cigar box, we were free to be *more* than just the documenting files of our past, and *less* than pie-eyed stories we tell ourselves about the future.

Tonight, under all that glistening wood, we dabbled in freedom.

Or maybe my brain is just overstimulated and reeling from being in the general vicinity of attractive women.

Maybe I'm just telling myself a story because that's what I do.

Maybe there is no profound meaning.

Or maybe the most profound meaning is that I may have never known what freedom felt like in the first place.

The emergency lights in 9-Block never go out. Their yellow halos run into the bars of my cell where they break up and stretch faint shadows across my ceiling. If I ever paint a picture up there I'll incorporate the patterns of light. A distorted chess board maybe.

I did learn one undeniable fact from that little white piece of paper tonight: If, after seven years of incarcerated stasis, you're unexpectedly painted back to life inside of an old prison cigar box by two college coeds, don't expect to get a full night's sleep.

Which, I guess, is a small price to pay to learn what freedom feels like, in the off chance I ever come across it again.

The plan is to erase us. They dig holes, surround them with bricks wrapped in razor wire and expect us to be forgotten. This is my refusal to go away. I am a pebble in the shoe of the prison industrial complex. My name is Robert Lee Allen Caldwell MDOC#929141.

Robert Boucheron is an architect in Charlottesville, Virginia. His short stories and essays are in *Bellingham Review, Fiction International, Louisville Review,* and *Saturday Evening Post.* His flash fiction is in online magazines.

Natalie Gerich Brabson is a graduate of Sarah Lawrence College's MFA program and holds a BA in Hispanic Studies from Vassar College. Her fiction has been published in *Cleaver Magazine, Philadelphia Stories, New World Writing,* and *Eunoia Review.* In 2017, she was selected as Go On Girl Book Club's Unpublished Writer Awardee. Born in Buffalo, she lives in West Philadelphia and is at work on her first novel.

William Burtch has recent work published in *American Fiction* Volume 17 (an anthology of New Rivers Press) and was a finalist for the American Fiction Short Story Award in 2018. His writing has appeared in journals and magazines both in print and online. He tweets at @WilliamBurtch2. More at: williamburtch.com

Robert Lee Allen Caldwell was born in Detroit but spent most of his youth in Florida. He now lives behind a wall in Michigan where he writes and does a podcast, Notes From The Pen, to spread awareness about the need for prison reform: https://podcasts.apple.com/us/podcast/notes-from-the-pen/id1518819034

In addition to *Schuylkill Valley Journal,* **Joe Cilluffo**'s poems have appeared in journals such as *Philadelphia Poets, Apiary,* and *Philadelphia Stories.* He was the Featured Poet for the Fall 2014 edition of *SVJ,* which has nominated two of Joe's poems, "Light" and "Forsythia," for the Pushcart Prize. *Philadelphia Stories* recently selected his poem, "Hospice," for their 15th Anniversary Edition. Joe's first book of poetry, *Always in the Wrong Season,* is available on Amazon.com.

Mike Cohen hosts Poetry Aloud and Alive at Philadelphia's Big Blue Marble Book Store. His articles on sculpture appear in *Schuylkill Valley Journal* in which he is a contributing editor. Mike has memorized a good deal of his poetry, having found that while some poems should be seen and not heard, others should be heard and not seen. It is a constant struggle to keep them sorted properly and to keep poems that should be neither seen nor heard out of the mix. Constant companion, cohabitant, cohort, and confidante, Connie, keeps Mike and his poems from getting off-kilter. Mike's wry writing has appeared in the *Mad Poets Review, Fox Chase Review,* and other journals. His poetic presentations feature humor and drama against a philosophical backdrop. Look for him at http://mikecohensays.com, on YouTube, and in his book, *Between the I's* as well as the forthcoming collection of poems and short tales, *Between the Shadow and the Wall.*

Arthur Davis has had over a hundred original tales published in eighty journals. He was featured in a single author anthology, nominated for a Pushcart Prize, received the 2018 Write Well Award for excellence in short fiction and, twice nominated, received Honorable Mention in *The Best American Mystery Stories 2017.*

Steve Denehan is the author of two chapbooks and two poetry collections. Twice winner of Irish Times' New Irish Writing, his numerous publication credits include *Poetry Ireland Review, Acumen, Prairie Fire, Westerly* and *Into the Void.* He has been nominated for Best of the Net, Best New Poet, and The Pushcart Prize.

Mike Dillon lives in Indianola, Washington, a small town on Puget Sound northwest of Seattle. He is the author of four books of poetry and three books of haiku. Several of his haiku were included in *Haiku in English: The First Hundred Years*, from W.W. Norton (2013). His most recent book, *Departures: Poetry and Prose on the Removal of Bainbridge Island's Japanese Americans after Pearl Harbor*, was published by Unsolicited Press in April 2019.

Jane Ebihara is a retired middle school literature teacher and the author of two chapbooks, *A Little Piece of Mourning* (Finishing Line Press, 2014) and *A Reminder of Hunger and Wings* (Finishing Line Press, 2019). She has been published in numerous literary journals and several anthologies, including *Tiferet, US 1 Worksheets, Adanna Literary Journal, Edison Literary Review* and *Sonic Boom* among others. She is an associate editor of *The Stillwater Review.*

W. D. Ehrhart's newest book is *Thank You for Your Service: Collected Poems*, McFarland & Company, Inc., 2019.

Christine M. Estel lives and writes in the Philadelphia area, and she tweets from @EstellingAStory.

Katherine Hahn Falk's poems have been recognized through publications and awards including an upcoming chapbook (Moonstone Press, 2021) and event commissions. She was Pennsylvania Poet Laureate for Bucks County in 2017. Recently, Katherine was one of four poets for *Radical Freedom: Poets on the Life and Work of H.D.*, and was an editor for *Fire Up The Poems*, an anthology of poetry prompts for HS teachers. She loves working with students on their poetry.

Lynn Fanok is the author of *Bread and Fumes* (Kelsay Books, 2021). Her collection explores the cultural influence of her father's Ukrainian heritage, and the complexities of being the daughter of a WWII labor camp survivor. Her poems have appeared in *Painted Bride Quarterly*, *Tiny Seed Journal*, *Red Wolf Press*, and a forthcoming poetry anthology, *Carry Us to the Next Well*. She has taught English literature courses, ESL, and leads a poetry series at an independent bookstore.

Catherine Findorak is a poet, fiction writer, and public librarian. She received an English degree from the University of Connecticut and an MSLIS from St. John's University. Her short fiction has previously been featured on The NoSleep Podcast.

Linda M. Fischer's poems have appeared in *Atlanta Review*, *Blue Heron Review*, *Ibbetson Street*, *Innisfree Poetry Journal*, *Iodine Poetry Journal*, *Poetry East*, *Potomac Review*, *Roanoke Review*, *Valparaiso Poetry Review*, *The Worcester Review*, and the anthology *Art Through the Eyes of Mad Poets*. She won the 2019 Philadelphia Writers' Conference Poetry Contest and recently published her 3rd chapbook, *Passages* (The Orchard Street Press). Her website: lindamfischer.com

Elizabeth Fletcher's poems have appeared in *Schuylkill Valley Journal*, *Tiny Seed Literary Journal*, *Ekphrastic Review*, *Ariel Chart*, and in the anthology *Lost Orchard* among others. Her nature essays on snowy owls and sea turtles have appeared in *The Philadelphia Inquirer*, and she is a co-author of medical education research publications. She has a BA from Hamilton College and an MS in Technical Communication from Drexel University.

Joseph E. Fleckenstein published over two dozen short stories and three books in addition to several other items. He is an army veteran, having been commander of a platoon of soldiers overseas. His website is at www.Writer-JEF.com.

Marsha Foss, a retired educator, divides her time between two states, Minnesota and Maryland. Her work has appeared in online and print journals in the United States, England, and Canada. Poems have been published in such places as *Your Daily Poem, Red Wing Arts Poet-Artist Collaboration, Ekphrasis, Friends Journal, Haiku Journal, The Talking Stick, Modern Poetry Quarterly Review, Halcyon*, and *Writing Magazine*. She has been nominated for a Pushcart Prize.

Jennifer L Freed has work appearing/forthcoming in various journals including *Atlanta Review, Atticus Review, Worcester Review*, and *Zone 3*, as well as in anthologies such as *Forgotten Women, a Tribute in Poetry* (Grayson Books). Her chapbook, *These Hands Still Holding*, was a finalist in the 2013 New Women's Voices contest. Her poem sequence "Cerebral Hemorrhage" won the 2020 Samuel Washington Allen prize from the New England Poetry club. jfreed.weebly.com

Nicole Greaves's poetry has appeared in numerous reviews and was awarded prizes by The Academy of American Poets and the Leeway Foundation of Philadelphia. She was a 2015 finalist for the Coniston Prize of Radar Poetry, who nominated her for The Best of the Net. She was a 2020 finalist for the Frontier Digital Chapbook and the Dogfish Head Poetry Contests. Poet laureate emeritus of Montgomery County, Pennsylvania, Nicole holds an MFA from Columbia University.

Karen Greenbaum-Maya is a retired clinical psychologist and former German major and writer of restaurant reviews, and a two-time Pushcart and Best of the Net nominee. Her first full sentence was, "Look at the moon!" Collections include *The Book of Knots and their Untying* (Kelsay Books) and the chapbooks *Burrowing Song, Eggs Satori*, and *Kafka's Cat* (Kattywompus Press). She co-curates Fourth Sundays, a poetry series in Claremont, California.

Ray Greenblatt published two books of poetry in 2020: *Until the First Light* (Parnilis Media) and *Man in a Crow Suit* (BookArts Press). He has also published Flash Fiction and book reviews. The Dylan Thomas Society, the John Updike Society, and the Graham Greene Society are the most recent publishers of his reviews. His work has been translated into Japanese, Polish, and Greek.

Eric Greinke has been active on the international literary scene since the early seventies. His poems and essays have been published in hundreds of magazines, most recently in *The American Journal of Poetry, Rosebud, North*

Dakota Quarterly, *Trajectory* and the *Bryant Literary Review*. His book *For The Living Dead – Selected Poems* (Presa Press & Simon Pulse, 2014) has been downloaded over three million times and was nominated for a Pulitzer Prize and a National Book Award. His new collection of poetry is *Break Out* (Presa Press, 2020). He has worked in the Michigan Artists In The Schools Program and as a creative writing teacher at Grand Rapids City School, an experimental public school. He has also been an active reviewer of over one hundred poetry books over the past fifty years. www.ericgreinke.com

John Grey is Australian born short storywriter, poet, playwright, musician. Has been published in numerous magazines including *Weird Tales*, *Christian Science Monitor*, *Greensboro Poetry Review*, *Poem*, *Agni*, *Poet Lore* and *Journal Of The American Medical Association*. His latest book is *Leaves On Pages* available through Amazon. Has had plays produced in Los Angeles and off-off Broadway in New York. Winner of Rhysling Award for short genre poetry in 1999.

Poet and storyteller **Luray Gross** is the author of four collections of poetry, most recently *Lift*, published by Ragged Sky Press of Princeton, NJ. She was awarded a Fellowship in Poetry by the New Jersey State Council on the Arts and named one of their Distinguished Teaching Artists. She has worked with thousands of students and teachers, as well as the general public, during thirty-some years as an Artist in Residence.

William Heath has published two chapbooks, *Night Moves in Ohio* and *Leaving Seville*; a book of poems, *The Walking Man*; three novels, *The Children Bob Moses Led* (winner of the Hackney Award), *Devil Dancer*, and *Blacksnake's Path*; a work of history, *William Wells and the Struggle for the Old Northwest* (winner of two Spur Awards); and a collection of interviews, *Conversations with Robert Stone*. www.williamheathbooks.com

Aiden Heung (He/They) is a Chinese poet born and raised on the edge of the Tibetan Plateau. His work has appeared or is forthcoming in *The Australian Poetry Journal*, *Cha*, *Poet Lore*, *Rust & Moth*, *Parentheses*, *Orison Anthology*, *Southern Humanities Review*, and *The Brooklyn Review* among many other places. He can be found on twitter @AidenHeung. Visit his website for more information: http://www.aidenheung.com/

Ray Keifetz is the author of *Night Farming In Bosnia*, winner of the Bitter Oleander Library of Poetry Award. His poems and stories have recently appeared or are forthcoming in *Gargoyle, I-70 Review, Kestrel, Osiris, Phantom Drift* and others. His work has received three Pushcart Prize nominations.

Nancy Smiler Levinson is author of *Moments of Dawn: A Poetic Memoir of Love & Family, Affliction & Affirmation*, as well as work that has appeared in numerous journals and anthologies including *Voice of Eve, Poetica, Panoply, Rat's Ass Journal, Constellations, Third Wednesday, The Copperfield Review, Sleet,* and elsewhere. In past chapters of her life she published some thirty books for young readers.

Joyce Meyers' poetry appears in *Atlanta Review, The Comstock Review, Slant, Iodine Poetry Journal,* and *Common Ground Review,* among others. Her published collections include *The Way Back* (Kelsay Books, 2017), and two chapbooks, *Wild Mushrooms* (Plan B, 2007) and *Shapes of Love* (Finishing Line, 2010). In 2014 she won the Atlanta Review Poetry Competition and was nominated for a Pushcart Prize.

Ann E. Michael, who directs the writing center at DeSales University, is the author of numerous chapbook collections of poetry and has had poems in print since the early 1980s. Her books include *Water-Rites, Barefoot Girls,* and the forthcoming collection *The Red Queen Hypothesis.*

Amy Suzanne Parker is a PhD student in Binghamton University's English and Creative Writing program. Her work is forthcoming in DIAGRAM and has appeared in *Pithead Chapel, Hobart, Entropy, Witch Craft Magazine, Burrow Press Review,* and elsewhere. Originally from the Tampa Bay Area, she loves a good storm.

Gloria Parker is a retired primary school teacher. Her poems have appeared in *Prairie Schooner, Margie, Mad Poets Review, Slipstream, Loch Raven Review, Rattle, Nimrod, Edison Literary Review,* South Florida Poetry Journal, *The Healing Muse, North of Oxford, Black Coffee Review,* and *Paterson Literary Review.*

Mark Robinson earned his BA in English Literature from the University of Iowa and is a MFA candidate at Lindenwood University. His poems have appeared in *Crab Creek Review, Exterminating Angel Press, Stillwater Review, Levee Magazine* and *Bending Genres,* among others. His chapbook *Just Last Days* was published in 2020. Mark currently lives in his hometown, Des Moines, IA.

Walter "Terry" Sanville lives in San Luis Obispo, California with his artist-poet wife (his in-house editor) and two plump cats (his in-house critics). He writes full time, producing short stories, essays, and novels. His short stories have been accepted more than 440 times by journals, magazines, and anthologies including *The Potomac Review*, *The Bryant Literary Review*, and *Shenandoah*. He was nominated twice for Pushcart Prizes and once for inclusion in Best of the Net anthology. Terry is a retired urban planner and an accomplished jazz and blues guitarist—who once played with a symphony orchestra backing up jazz legend George Shearing.

Nikki Williams is a multimedia journalist and writer. Her work appears in *The Citron Review*, *Ellipsiszine*, *Sublunary Review*, *LEON Literary Review*, *Literary Yard* and is forthcoming in HOOT and PreeLit. She munches trail mix and takes stunning photos when not busy writing. She's still figuring out Twitter at: @ohsashalee / See more: linktr.ee/writenowrong

Francine Witte's poetry and fiction have appeared in *Smokelong Quarterly*, *Wigleaf*, *Mid-American Review*, and *Passages North*. Her latest books are *Dressed All Wrong for This* (Blue Light Press), *The Way of the Wind* (AdHoc fiction), and *The Theory of Flesh*. Her chapbook, *The Cake, The Smoke, The Moon* (flash fiction) will be published by ELJ September, 2021. She is flash fiction editor for *Flash Boulevard* and *The South Florida Poetry Journal*. She lives in NYC.

John Wojtowicz grew up working on his family's azalea and rhododendron nursery in the backwoods of what Ginsberg dubbed "nowhere Zen New Jersey." Currently, he works as a clinical social worker and adjunct professor. He also serves as the Local Lyrics contributor for the Mad Poet Society blog. Recent publications include: *Kansas City Voices*, *West Trade Review*, *Tule Review*, *Toho*, *Glassworks*, *Paterson Literary Review* and *The Poeming Pigeon*. Find out more at: www.catfishjohnpoetry.com

Daniel A. Zehner wrote poems and haiku for his own enjoyment during most of his 49-year career as a trial lawyer, mostly in New Jersey. Encouraged by a poet/friend, in 2014 he began submitting to journals. His poems and haiku have appeared in *Paterson Literary Review*, *the Aurorean*, *Frogpond* and the following Moonstone Press journals: *Philadelphia Says: Not Our President*, *Philadelphia Says: Haiku*, *On War and Peace*, and *Not Our President: Volume 2*.

.

Peter Krok

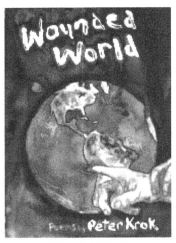

Wounded World
$10.00 (ISBN 978-1-946150-65-3)

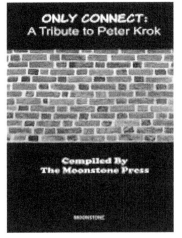

Only Connect: A Tribute to Peter Krok
$10.00 (ISBN 978-1-946150-71-4)

Peter Krok has been the Editor-in-Chief of the *Schuylkill Valley Journal* since 2001. He also is the humanities/poetry director of the Manayunk Roxborough Art Center where he has coordinated a literary series since 1990. Because of his identification with row house and red brick Philadelphia, he is often referred to as "the red brick poet." His poems have appeared in the *Yearbook of American Poetry, America, Mid-America Poetry Review, Midwest Quarterly, Poet Lore, Potomac Review, Blue Unicorn* and numerous other print and online journals. In 2005 his poem "10 PM At a Philadelphia Recreation Center" was included in *Common Wealth: Contemporary Poets on Pennsylvania* (published by Penn State University). He is author of *Looking For An Eye* (2008, Foothills Press) and *Wounded World* (2020, The Moonstone Press).

Only Connect features poems of praise and appreciation by 45 poets who have worked with Peter over the years, including many contributors and editorial staff of *SVJ*.

Books are available at
www.moonstoneartscenter.org

"Only connect! That was the whole of her sermon. Only connect the prose and the passion, and both will be exalted, and human love will be seen at its height. Live in fragments no longer."
 –E.M. Forster, Howards End

Schuylkill Valley Journal

—Submission Guidelines—

Schuylkill Valley Journal is published as both a print and online journal. *SVJ* print is released twice a year, in spring and fall. *SVJ* online (svjlit.com) is published on a more frequent basis. *SVJ* publishes short stories, flash fiction, interviews, photography, cityscapes, critical essays and features on art and sculpture (especially Philadelphia sculpture). *SVJ* also publishes poetry; however, all poetry will first appear in *SVJ* print.

All submissions (except poetry) should be sent through the website to svj.query@gmail.com. Please see separate information for poetry below. We prefer previously unpublished work though published work is acceptable (indicate where previously published). Simultaneous submissions are OK (please notify us if your work is published elsewhere). All submissions will be considered for both our print and online journals. Our aim in reviewing material that is first considered for *SVJ* online (material other than poetry and longer short stories) is to inform writers of the status of their inquiry within two weeks.

Submissions should be sent in .doc or .rtf file format only in Times New Roman, 12-point font, and single-spaced and should include title, author name, bio and complete text, including any notes regarding previous publication. In the subject line all submissions should state the submission type (e.g., short story, flash fiction, essay) and include the writer's full name, and contact information. Any file not meeting these specifications may not be read. Manuscripts will not be returned. All submissions except poetry should include a word count.

Poetry: Because of the high volume of poetry we receive, we have both a separate submission address and different guidelines from our other genres. Please visit our website to read all Poetry guidelines before submitting, and send poems directly to the poetry editor, Bernadette McBride, at PoetrySVJ@gmail.com.

Short Stories and Flash Fiction: 1-2 stories (if more than 3,000 words please only submit one). Flash fiction (preferably 500-1,000 words); short stories no more than 6,000 words. Submissions will be considered for both the online and print journal, with the exception of short stories greater than 2,000 words (*SVJ* print only). We like fiction that explores a situation or illuminates a character. We look for original use of language, fresh voices, and diversity. We also seek writers who have insights into the mysteries of everyday life, relationships and the world around us. Stories can pose questions and answer them or not; however, they must be well-crafted. Stories can be sent through the website to query.svj@gmail.com or can be sent via snail mail. The preferred method is via snail mail. Stories sent by snail mail should be typed, double-spaced, one side only with name, address, word count and bio on first page. Send to:

> Fran Metzman
> Fiction Editor, *Schuylkill Valley Journal*
> 1900 JFK Blvd, /2012
> Philadelphia, PA 19103

Essays and Interviews: 5,000 words max. (preferably under 2,000 words for *SVJ* online) on topics of literary or artistic interest, personal reflections, interviews, etc.). Submissions should incude the word count and bio on first page. Inquiry to email address (macpoet1@aol.com) is always advisable. Queries should include a concept/abstract of the proposed article, approximately a paragraph. All submissions will be sent through query.svj@gmail.com. All articles and non-fiction pieces will be assigned by editor.

Dispatches: Send 250-700 words + 50 word bio to dispatchsvj@gmail.com & feel free to add one link to your work / website that we will include with your bio. Dispatches is genre free. Whether it's beautiful or it's weird, we don't care as long as you keep it loose.

—Copyright—

Material that appears in *Schuylkill Valley Journal* (print and online) is the copyright of the contributor. By submitting a work to SVJ, the contributor agrees that *SVJ* reserves first rights, and the right to retain the material in our archives indefinitely. It may also be used in reference to previous issues and be included in future *SVJ* endeavors. All other rights belong to the contributor. *SVJ* online does not claim ownership of syndicated material from other sources, and proper credit will be given as necessary. We request the same courtesy from our peers. All rights are similarly reserved by *Schuylkill Valley Journal*.

—Payment—

For contributors to *SVJ* print, payment is one copy of the journal in which your work appears. Additional copies are $10 each. All rights revert to authors upon publication. The cost of *Schuylkill Valley Journal* is $10 an issue and $13 if sent via mail domestically. For other information about SVJ, contact Peter Krok, the publisher and Editor-in-Chief of *SVJ*, and Humanities Director of the Manayunk-Roxborough Art Center (MRAC), at macpoet1@aol.com or by phone at 215-482-3363 (MRAC) or 610-609-1490 (cell).

—Subscription Form—
Schuylkill Valley Journal

Name: _____

Street Address:_____

City, State, Zip Code:_____

Phone: _____

Subscriptions: ( ) One Year $23*   ( ) Two Years $45*
                   (includes postage)   (includes postage)

For an issue that contains my work:

( ) Send my payment copies with my subscription copy.

( ) Send my payment copies and transfer my subscription
     to the next issue.

Contributions
     ( ) $10   ( ) $25   ( ) $50   ( ) $100   ( ) Other

Please make checks payable to
     Peter Krok – *Schuylkill Valley Journal*
and mail to:
     Peter Krok, 240 Golf Hills Road, Havertown, PA 19083

*For subscriptions that do not require postage, a one year subscription is $20 and a two year subscription is $40.

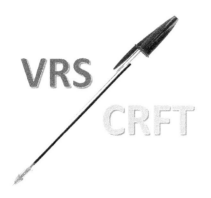

Made in the USA
Monee, IL
04 September 2021